The Economic Theory of Price Indices

ECONOMIC THEORY AND MATHEMATICAL ECONOMICS

Consulting Editor: Karl Shell

UNIVERSITY OF PENNSYLVANIA
PHILADELPHIA, PENNSYLVANIA

Franklin M. Fisher and Karl Shell. **The Economic Theory of Price Indices:** *Two Essays on the Effects of Taste, Quality, and Technological Change.*

In preparation

Luis Eugenio Di Marco (Ed.). **International Economics and Development:** *Essays in Honor of Raul Presbisch.*

Erwin Klein. **Mathematical Methods in Theoretical Economics:** *Topological and Vector Space Foundations of Equilibrium Analysis.*

The Economic Theory of Price Indices.

TWO ESSAYS ON THE EFFECTS OF TASTE, QUALITY, AND TECHNOLOGICAL CHANGE

FRANKLIN M. FISHER / KARL SHELL

Massachusetts Institute of Technology
Cambridge, Massachusetts

University of Pennsylvania
Philadelphia, Pennsylvania

ACADEMIC PRESS   New York and London   1972

ACADEMIC PRESS, INC.
111 Fifth Avenue, New York, New York 10003

United Kingdom Edition published by
ACADEMIC PRESS, INC. (LONDON) LTD.
24/28 Oval Road, London NW1

LIBRARY OF CONGRESS CATALOG CARD NUMBER: 77-187250

PRINTED IN THE UNITED STATES OF AMERICA

In Memory of
MIGUEL SIDRAUSKI

Contents

PREFACE ix

ACKNOWLEDGMENTS xv

ESSAY I

TASTE AND QUALITY CHANGE IN THE PURE THEORY OF THE TRUE COST-OF-LIVING INDEX

I. Introduction	1
II. The Theory of the True Cost-of-Living Index and Intertemporal Comparison of Welfare	2
III. Taste Change	7
IV. New Goods and Other Corner Solutions	22
V. Quality Change	26
Footnotes for Essay I	37
References for Essay I	44

ESSAY II

THE PURE THEORY OF THE NATIONAL OUTPUT DEFLATOR

I. Introduction	49
II. Real Output Indices and Production Possibility Maps	50
III. Which Index Is Relevant?	56
IV. Paasche and Laspeyres Indices	57
V. Market Imperfections and Underutilized Resources	59
VI. The Indices: Formal Description	61
VII. Hicks-Neutral Technological Change	63
VIII. Changing Factor Supplies and Factor-Augmenting Technological Change: The Two-Sector Model	75
IX. Changing Factor Supplies and Factor-Augmenting Technological Change: The General Case	81

Contents

X. Factor-Augmenting Technological Change in a Single Sector
of the Two-Sector Model   93
XI. General Technological Change   97
XII. New Goods, Disappearing Goods, and Corner Solutions   99
XIII. Quality Changes   105
Footnotes for Essay II   107
References for Essay II   113

INDEX   115

Given the complexity of the contemporary economy it is useful to summarize the increasingly abundant economic data in the form of selected indices. Examples include Gross National Product and the corresponding GNP deflator, the Consumer Price Index (CPI), the Dow-Jones stock market indices, and so forth. Economic indices, once constructed, often seem to possess lives of their own. The economist, however, in evaluating the usefulness of these indices must first consider the grounding of them in basic economic theory. The need for such a grounding in theory should always be obvious, but is often most apparent when a given index must be adapted to a changed or different environment or extended to include cases previously unconsidered.

In our first essay, we study the pure theory of the true cost-of-living index, which may be considered as an idealization of indices like the consumer price index and others of that type. It is now accepted by economists that cost-of-living indices are properly grounded in the theory of consumer demand. It is our purpose here to analyze the effects on the true cost-of-living index of changes in consumer taste, quality changes in purchased goods, and the introduction of new goods into the market place.

The definition of the true cost-of-living index depends crucially upon the choice of a single indifference map. Suppose we want to compare two hypothetical situations, A and B. If the prices prevailing in situation A differ from the prices prevailing in situation B, then we may want to deflate actual money income in situation B in order to make it comparable to money income in situation A. Given a fixed indifference map, we then ask how much income the consumer in B would require to make him just indifferent between facing prices prevailing in B and facing prices prevailing in A with a stated income. The income we have solved for divided by the stated income in situation A is then a true cost-of-living index which can be used for deflating situation B income.

In practice, however, the cost-of-living index is meant to compare two real situations (for example, yesterday and today) rather than two hypothetical ones (for example, A and B). It is also the case that the choice of the indifference map is not likely to be completely arbitrary. In the two–time-period case, the analyst will probably limit his choice to yesterday's or today's indifference map.

If he does so limit his choice, the analyst may also carelessly allow himself to be drawn into thinking in terms quite unwarranted by the theory and to carelessly speak as though the question answered by the true cost-of-living index were that of how much income would be required to make the consumer just as well off today as he was yesterday. If that were indeed the question which the true cost-of-living index answers, then it would be apparent that no meaning could be attached to such an index when tastes change. In fact, we argue that such a view is quite wrong and that such a question has no meaning whether or not tastes change. The question which the true cost-of-living index can answer is the perfectly meaningful one already indicated—how much income would be required to make the consumer just indifferent between facing the opportunities he actually faced yesterday and those which he would face today with today's prices and the stated income.

The latter question turns out to be a meaningful one (indeed, two meaningful ones) when tastes change, and we are thus able to examine such cases. We show that if one is merely willing to state that tastes do change without parametrizing the way in which such change takes place, then the Paasche price index will be a more reliable guide to the true cost-of-living index than will the Laspeyres index, the relation of the latter to the true index being lost. This suggests that lacking such a parametrization, the consumer price index should be computed as a Paasche index, contrary to the usual practice.

If one is willing to parametrize taste change, however, then one can go farther and, among other things, analyze the way in which a Laspeyres index should be altered. Accordingly, we work out a particular example rather completely, taking the case of taste changes which can be parametrized as good-augmenting. It is argued that this may be an appropriate parametrization of the learning process which occurs when goods have been recently introduced.

The question of how a new good itself should be handled is also studied by allowing for corner solutions in the general analysis. We are able to close a gap in the existing literature and to show that the appropriate price with which a new good should be credited before its appearance is not indeterminate but is the demand reservation price (the intercept on the demand curve). We remark, however, that this problem is strictly speaking relevant only to the construction of a Paasche index (or a Laspeyres index in the case of a disappearing good) and arises only indirectly in the theory of the true cost-of-living index itself.

In practice, quality change is handled in the Consumer Price Index by assuming that an improvement in quality in a given good is equivalent to a price reduction in that good. We argue that while there are cases where this is the appropriate general treatment, other cases exist in which this approach is not so satisfactory. We show that an own-price adjustment made independently of the amount of all goods purchased is an appropriate adjustment if and only if the only effect of quality change is of the good-augmenting type. While an adjustment in the price of the good whose quality is changing can always be made to suffice locally (that is, for given purchases of all goods), in general the price adjustment which must be made will depend on all prices and purchases of all commodities and not simply on the physical characteristics of the quality change. It is hardly necessary to add that adjustments made in practice do not satisfy this condition, nor do the more sophisticated treatments in the "hedonic" price index literature.

While it has been long recognized that the economic theory of the cost-of-living index is based upon the theory of consumer demand, it seems to be less generally agreed that the construction of national-output deflators ought to be similarly grounded in the economic theory of production. In our second essay we attempt to provide this grounding and consequently attempt to provide a foundation for the measurement of real national output (or product). Our theory turns out to be isomorphic to that of the cost-of-living index with a construction called the "production possibility map" replacing the indifference map. (Many of the above results can thus be carried over with appropriate reinterpretation.) It is shown that the usual inequalities relating Paasche and Laspeyres to the true index are reversed (from what they are in cost-of-living theory) for the case of production.

We then go on to examine the implications of changing production possibilities—changes which come about either because of technological change or because of a change of factor supplies. It is shown that unless one is willing to parametrize such a change, the GNP deflator should be computed as a Laspeyres index in practice—contrary to the usual custom but parallel to the similar result for the consumer price index for which we argued in Essay I the choice between Paasche and Laspeyres is also wrongly made in practice. The case of Hicks-neutral change is worked out in detail, advantage often being taken of the isomorphism between the theory of the GNP deflator and the theory developed in Essay I for the cost-of-living index.

Special attention is focused on technological change in the simple two-sector production model of Rybczynski and Uzawa. We investigate two formally equivalent cases: (1) that in which the relevant supply of factors changes from period to period (or situation to situation) and (2) that in which technological change is purely factor-augmenting and does not depend upon the sector in which the factor is employed. The "correction" that must be made to account for changed technology depends upon two things: (1) the direction of movement over time of the capital–labor ratio in efficiency units and (2) relative capital intensities in the two sectors.

We also analyze the effects upon the real national-output deflator of the general case of changing factor supplies and factor-augmenting change. Few very practical results are developed, since in multisectoral models it is not at all straightforward to derive basic conditions for such phenomena as a rise in the price of the ith good leading to an increase in the share of the mth factor. However, some fairly elegant and interesting theorems can be proved. Further results can be obtained, moreover, for the case of factor-augmenting technological change in a single sector of the two-sector model. The effect of such technological change upon the real national-output deflator depends not only upon relative capital intensities in the two sectors, but also on the production elasticities of substitution in each of the two sectors.

Results on the treatment of new goods and of quality change are also obtained, making heavy use of the isomorphism with the theory of Essay I. In particular, we show that the *supply* reservation price (the intercept on the supply curve) is the correct one to use in dealing with new or disappearing goods. We also show that the usual type of correction for quality change will be correct only if the production of the new variety of the given good embodies the same resources in fixed proportions as a fixed quantity of the original variety—in effect, the two production functions differing by a Hicks-neutral technological change. This is obviously a very restrictive condition.

Proofs of theorems and lemmas in our second essay are generally less complicated and detailed than the proofs in the first essay. This, of course, is largely because we are able, for purposes of proof, to exploit the theorems proved in Essay I because of the fundamental isomorphism. In Essay I, the important theorems are developed from lemmas that we feel expose many interesting aspects of the underlying economic structure of the model. In Essay II, we chose a more economical method of proof, relying on the general envelope theorem[1] rather than redeveloping special instances for our theory.

[1] See, for example, Samuelson (1947, p. 32). The envelope theorem states that in the neighborhood of an optimum the *ceteris paribus* change in the optimized quantity, due to a first-order change in some underlying parameter, is equal to its *mutatis mutandis* change.

Acknowledgments

We are grateful to the Federal Reserve Board Committee on Prices and Price Measurement for support of our research underlying the first essay. This essay is a slightly revised version of a paper with the same title originally appearing in *Value, Capital, and Growth: Papers in Honour of Sir John Hicks* (edited by J. N. Wolfe) (1968). We are also grateful to Edinburgh University Press for allowing us to use the paper here. We are indebted to Paul A. Samuelson and Robert Summers for helpful discussions but we retain responsibility for error. We are indebted to the National Science Foundation for grants to M.I.T. and the University of Pennsylvania for support of research which led to the second essay. A highly condensed version of this essay was presented to the Second World Congress of the Econometric Society (Cambridge, 1970) but is published here in its entirety for the first time. We are indebted to Robert M. Solow for helpful discussions, but again we retain responsibility for error.

Taste and Quality Change in the
Pure Theory of the True Cost-of-Living Index

I. *Introduction*

The standard theory of the true cost-of-living index gives a rather uncomfortable treatment to taste and quality changes (including the introduction of new goods). The consumer is assumed to have always had an unchanging indifference map, complete with axes for all new goods of whose potential existence he in fact was not aware before their introduction. Similarly, quality change is treated either as an introduction of a new good or as a simple repackaging of an old one equivalent to a price reduction.[1] Yet the justification for the latter procedure has never been satisfactorily set forth, while the former one meets with many of the same difficulties as does the treatment of new goods itself.

If the treatment of new goods and quality change is less than fully satisfactory, however, the treatment of taste change is nonexistent. The assumption of an unchanging indifference map even defined over nonexistent goods is apparently crucial for a theory which is often erroneously thought to answer the question: How much would it cost in today's prices to make the consumer just as well off as he was yesterday? This question cannot be answered without resorting to an arbitrary intertemporal weighting of utilities. Yet taste changes do occur and the cost-of-living index is often carelessly thought to be designed to answer that question (Nat. Bur. Econ. Res., 1961, pp. 51–9; v. Hofsten, 1952).

This essay begins by arguing that the difficulty is due only to a misinterpretation of the theory of the true cost-of-living index. That theory does not in fact seek to answer the question posed above, nor does it make intertemporal comparisons of utility. Indeed, we observe that such a question can never be answered and such comparisons never made because they have no operational content. Incautious application of the theory has avoided facing up to this by the use of an apparently appealing but completely arbitrary and untestable hidden assumption which does no apparent harm when tastes are constant but which breaks down utterly when tastes do change.

That assumption, however, is not part of the theory and the question which the theory does answer retains its meaning whether or not tastes are constant. The pure theory of the cost-of-living index, rigorously interpreted, accommodates taste changes quite comfortably.

Accordingly, we then go on to consider a case of parametrizable taste change in full detail. That case can be given the interpretation of consumers learning more about the properties of a recently introduced good. We derive the consequences for index number construction of such a circumstance.

Moreover, the rigorous formulation of the theory involved in the treatment of taste change aids also in the treatment of new goods and of quality change. It does so in two ways. First, the formally acceptable but practically uncomfortable assumption that the consumer has always known about unavailable goods and qualities disappears. Second, by focusing attention on a proper question, the analysis of new goods and quality change becomes relatively straightforward. While it is true in principle that (unlike the case of taste change) the same analysis could be carried out without so rigorous a formulation (given the assumption of unchanging tastes for nonexistent goods), that formulation makes it very clear what is involved. Asking the right question is a good part of obtaining the answer.

Thus the last two sections of the essay discuss the treatment of new goods and of quality change respectively and show what kind of information is needed for the handling of these problems in a satisfactory manner.

II. *The Theory of the True Cost-of-Living Index and*
Intertemporal Comparisons of Welfare

As indicated, a frequently encountered view of the true cost-of-living index is that it is designed to answer the question: 'What income would be required to make a consumer faced with today's prices just as well off as he was yesterday when he faced yesterday's income and yesterday's prices?' The difficulty that is presented by taste changes in answering this question is immediately apparent. What is meant by 'just as well off as he was yesterday' if the indifference map has shifted?

Yet reflection on this issue shows that the same difficulty appears even if tastes do not change. While it is apparently natural to say that a man whose tastes have remained constant is just as well off today as he was yesterday if he is on the same indifference curve in both periods, the appeal of that proposition is no more than apparent. In both periods, the man's utility function is determined only up to a monotonic transformation; how can we possibly know whether the level of true utility (whatever that may mean) corresponding to a given indifference curve is the same in both periods? The man's efficiency as a pleasure-machine may have changed without changing his tastes.

Indeed, we have no more justification for saying that a man on the same indifference curve at two different times is equally well off at both than we do for saying that two men who happen to have the same indifference map are equally well off if they have the same possessions. Both statements are attractive for reasons of simplicity and both are completely without any operational content whatsoever. One never steps into the same river twice and the comparison between a man's utility now and his utility yesterday stands on precisely the same lack of footing as the comparison of the utilities of two different men.

Thus, a consideration of the problem of taste change on this interpretation of the theory of the true cost-of-living index merely makes explicit a problem that is apparently there all the time. If that theory were really founded upon intertemporal comparisons of utility of the type described, then that theory would be without foundation.[2]

In fact, however, the theory of the true cost-of-living index makes no such comparisons, and rigorous statements of that theory have avoided them. Such statements run as follows: 'Given an indifference map, we compare two *hypothetical* situations, A and B. We ask how much income the consumer in B would require to make him just indifferent between facing B's prices and facing A's prices with a stated income.' Note that the question of whether the consumer has the same utility in A as in B never arises. So long as we remain on this level of abstraction, the point in time and space at which the consumer has the indifference map used in the comparison may be A or it may be B or it may be any other *single* point different from both of these.

In practice, however, the cost-of-living index is meant to compare two real situations rather than two hypothetical ones and A and B become, for example, yesterday and today, respectively. In this case, it is natural to take the indifference map to be used as the one in force at either A or B,[3] and if tastes have not changed so that the two maps are the same, it is easy to slip into the erroneous (but in this case harmless) usage of saying that what is compared are the relative costs of making the consumer at B just as well off as he was at A. If the indifference maps differ, however, such a slip is dangerous and it must never be forgotten that the viewpoint from which the comparison is made is not necessarily identical with either A or B.

Thus, the true cost-of-living index is supposed to represent a comparison between two opportunity or constraint loci not between two utility levels. The first constraint locus is that given by yesterday's income and prices – it is yesterday's budget constraint. The second is a budget constraint defined by today's prices but with income a parameter. The true cost-of-living index does not answer the question: 'How much income would it take today to make me as well off as I was yesterday with yesterday's budget constraint?' That question is unanswerable. A similar-seeming question which *can* be answered is: 'How much income is required *today* to make me just indifferent between facing yesterday's budget constraint and facing a budget constraint defined by today's prices and the income in question?' The latter question refers to a choice which can in principle be posed; the former does not.

Note further that the question just posed retains its meaning even if tastes have changed between yesterday and today. It is a question posed entirely in terms of today's tastes and involves a comparison of present and past *constraints*, not a comparison of present and past utilities. As it were, we replace the question: 'Were you happier when young than you are now?' with the question: 'Would you like to live your youth over again, having the tastes you do now?' The latter question may seem more fanciful than the former, but it is the one which is operationally meaningful.

It is evident, however, that a second question can also be posed, the answer to which may differ from that to the question just suggested if tastes in fact change. That question is: 'What income would have been required *yesterday* to make you just indifferent between facing yesterday's budget constraint and facing a budget constraint defined by today's prices and the income in question?' This is the same question as before from the vantage of yesterday's tastes rather than today's. It is equally meaningful, but, we shall argue below, not as interesting.[4]

If tastes do not change, then the answers to the two questions coincide.

In this case also, it is obvious that the required income is precisely that income which would place the consumer today on the same indifference curve as he achieved yesterday. Thus, in the case of no taste change, the cost-of-living index implied by the answers to our questions is precisely that given by the erroneous application of the traditional theory. As indicated in the introduction, however, even in the case of no taste change the advantage of a rigorous formulation is more than aesthetic, since, by focusing attention on a choice between alternative constraints, such a formulation aids in the treatment of problems such as the incorporation of new goods or quality change into the cost-of-living index.

What about the case of taste change, however, in which we have asked two parallel but different questions which (in this case) have two different answers in general? It seems clear that when intertemporal problems are involved, the asymmetry of time makes the question asked assuming today's tastes more relevant than the equally meaningful question asked assuming yesterday's tastes.[5] That this is so may be seen from the following example.

Consider two alternative time paths of prices with the same initial values. In the first, path A, the cost-of-living index considered from the point of view of yesterday's tastes rises, while that considered from the point of view of current tastes stays constant or falls; in the second, path B, the reverse is true. It is clear that the consumer will be better off in every period under path A than under path B, or, equivalently, that in every period, the cost-of-living is higher on path B than on path A. Faced with a choice, rational policy should prefer path A to path B.[6] Indeed, every practical question which one wants the cost-of-living index to answer is answered with reference to current, not base-year tastes. Succinctly, if the prices of goods no longer desired rise and those of goods newly desired fall, a cost-of-living index should fall, not rise. The question of how a man with base-year tastes would view the matter is an operationally meaningful one; it is not a terribly relevant one, however, save insofar as it casts light on the cost of living viewed with current tastes.

This argument has an immediate corollary. The general practice in the construction of consumer price indices is to use Laspeyres indices with base-period quantity weights rather than Paasche indices with current weights. In the case of no taste change, a frequently encountered proposition is that a Laspeyres index overstates price rises and a Paasche index

understates them, because of the inadequate treatment afforded substitution effects.[7] If tastes change, however, and if we agree that it is the
current-taste cost-of-living in which we are interested, a Laspeyres index
loses much of its meaning. That index is a relevant upper bound for a
true cost-of-living index with base-year tastes; it need not be such a bound
for a true cost-of-living index with current tastes. A Paasche index, on the
other hand, retains its property of being a lower bound on the current-
tastes index (but may lose it for the base-year-taste index). When tastes
change, Laspeyres and Paasche indices cease to become approximations
to the same thing and become approximations to different things. As we
have just seen, it is the Paasche index which approximates the relevant
magnitude; the Laspeyres index becomes less relevant.

Indeed, such relevance as is retained by a Laspeyres index occurs only
if taste changes take place in such a way as to make a base-year-taste
index differ from a current-taste index in some specific way. If one is willing
to specify *how* tastes change and to parametrize that specification, one
may obtain results on how a Laspeyres index should be adjusted. This is
done for a specific class of cases in the next section. If one is not willing
to make such a specification, but believes that important taste changes
have taken place, one should put more reliance on a Paasche index and
less on a Laspeyres than has traditionally been done.[8]

Before closing this section, it may be well to formalize the question
which, we have argued, the true cost-of-living index is designed to answer.
Given base-period prices of goods $\hat{p}_1, \hat{p}_2, ..., \hat{p}_n$, base-period income $\hat{y}$,
current prices of goods $p_1, p_2, ..., p_n$, the problem is to find that income y
such that the representative consumer is *currently* indifferent between
facing current prices with income y and facing base-period prices with
base-period income. The true cost-of-living index is then $(y/\hat{y})$.

Let $u(\cdot)$ be an ordinal utility function derived from the representative
consumer's current preference map. The problem reduces to solving for
the nonnegative values of $x_1, x_2, ..., x_n$, that minimize the expression

$$y = p_1 x_1 + p_2 x_2 + \ldots + p_n x_n, \tag{2.1}$$

where x_i $(i = 1, 2, ..., n)$ is the amount of the ith good that would be purchased at current prices and income y, subject to the requirement that

$$u(x_1, x_2, \ldots, x_n) = u(\hat{x}_1, \hat{x}_2, \ldots, \hat{x}_n). \tag{2.2}$$

$\hat{x}_i$ $(i = 1, 2, \ldots, n)$ is the amount of the ith good that currently would be purchased if the consumer faced base-period prices with base-period income. That is, nonnegative $\hat{x}_1, \hat{x}_2, \ldots, \hat{x}_n$ are chosen to maximize utility

$$u(\hat{x}_1, \hat{x}_2, \ldots, \hat{x}_n) \tag{2.3}$$

subject to the budget constraint

$$\hat{y} \geqslant \hat{p}_1 \hat{x}_1 + \hat{p}_2 \hat{x}_2 + \ldots + \hat{p}_n \hat{x}_n . \tag{2.4}$$

It may be noted that a more compact formulation can be given in terms of the indirect utility function (Houthakker, 1951–2, 157–63). Thus, let $\phi(p_1, p_2, \ldots, p_n, y)$ be the indirect utility function, so that $\phi(p_1, p_2, \ldots, p_n, y)$ is the maximal value of $u(x_1, x_2, \ldots, x_n)$ subject to $\sum_1^n p_i x_i = y$. The cost-of-living index is $(y/\hat{y})$, where y is the solution to $\phi(p_1, p_2, \ldots, p_n, y) = \phi(\hat{p}_1, \hat{p}_2, \ldots, \hat{p}_n, \hat{y})$. We have not used this formulation in what follows since taste changes seem to be parametrizable more easily in terms of the direct than in terms of the indirect utility function and because we shall later work with more complicated constraints. However, the properties of the indirect utility function may be useful for future work in this area.

III. *Taste Change*
Consumers' tastes change for a variety of reasons some of which are so mysterious to the ordinary economist that he is unlikely to offer much in the way of a systematic understanding. But certain instances of taste change possess a more systematic structure. For example, it may be known to be the case that a recently introduced electrical appliance, say, increases monotonically in desirability through time during the period in which consumers are learning about the usefulness of the appliance. In such a case, one unit of the appliance in a later year may afford the same service as more than one in an earlier year because of the increase in consumer information but with no physical change in the good itself.

Certain goods seem to suffer similar losses in desirability through time. Dairy products, for which publicity about their possible relationship to certain circulatory diseases has been increasing through time, might be considered to have suffered a systematic decline in desirability to consumers.

These examples raise the important question of just what we mean by a taste change as opposed to a quality change. To take a slightly different idealized case, suppose that consumers suddenly learn to use a certain fuel more efficiently, getting a certain number of BTUs out of a smaller quantity of fuel. If the relevant axis on the indifference map is the amount of fuel *purchased*, then there has been a taste change; if it is the number of BTUs gained from such fuel, there has not been a taste change but a quality change – a change in the opportunities available to consumers. The change can be consistently treated in either way, but the two treatments will differ. When the phenomenon is treated as a quality change, the true cost-of-living index will decline; when it is analyzed as a taste change, this will not be the case. The decision turns on whether the cost of living should be said to decrease just because consumers are better at consuming. If we are concerned with the delivery to the consumer of certain 'basic satisfactions', a quality change is involved; this is an extension of the position taken in the construction of hedonic price indices. If, on the other hand, we are concerned with the valuation of opportunities *as available in the market*, then treatment of the change as being one of tastes is more appropriate. Both positions are tenable and both can lead to uncomfortable results if pushed to absurdity. (Suppose on the one hand that the new technique is discovered and popularized by fuel sellers. Suppose, on the other, that there is no change in the technology of fuel use but that people decide they now prefer a lower temperature in their houses.) The present section treats taste changes, the quality change case which is similarly parametrizable being treated in section v.

In this section, the case in which taste change may be parametrized as solely good-augmenting is treated in detail. A taste change is said to be good-augmenting if and only if the preference maps can be represented by a utility function whose ith argument is a function of the amount of purchases of the ith good and of the level of some taste change parameter.[9] Following the terminology employed in capital theory, we might call a taste change which is independent of any change in the qualities of the goods a disembodied taste change. In this section, the effect of such taste change upon the value of the true cost-of-living index is studied. We derive results in terms of the parameters of the demand functions which are, in particular, capable of being estimated from market data.

For convenience, assume that only one good, say the first, experiences an own-augmenting disembodied taste change. (Immediate generalization of the results to the case where more than one of the n goods experience own-augmenting disembodied taste changes is discussed at the end of this section.) Let the representative consumer's utility function be given by $u(bx_1, x_2, \ldots, x_n)$, where b is the parameter representing first-good-augmenting taste change and x_i ($i = 1, 2, \ldots, n$) is the amount of the ith good that is purchased.[10] Also assume that $u(\cdot)$ is an increasing, twice differentiable, strictly quasi-concave function which is defined over the nonnegative orthant of an n-dimensional space.[11] For the purposes of this section we also assume that all relevant maxima and minima are given by interior solutions to the first-order conditions. Corner solutions are treated in section IV.

We now turn to the formal analysis of the problem. If with current tastes the representative consumer faces base period income $\hat{y}$ and base period prices $\hat{p}$ where $\hat{p}$ is an n-dimensional column vector defined by $\hat{p}' = (\hat{p}_1, \hat{p}_2, \ldots, \hat{p}_n)$, his purchases would have been given by the column vector $\hat{x}$ which is defined by $\hat{x}' = (\hat{x}_1, \hat{x}_2, \ldots, \hat{x}_n)$. $\hat{p}_i$ and $\hat{x}_i$ ($i = 1, 2, \ldots, n$) are respectively the base period price of the ith good and the amount of the ith good that *would have been* purchased if he had faced the base period constraints with current tastes. $\hat{x}$ is found by solving the system of first-order conditions:

$$
\begin{pmatrix} \hat{p}'\hat{x} \\ b\hat{u}_1 \\ \hat{u}_2 \\ \cdot \\ \cdot \\ \cdot \\ \hat{u}_n \end{pmatrix} - \begin{pmatrix} \hat{y} \\ --- \\ \hat{\lambda}\hat{p} \end{pmatrix} = 0 , \tag{3.1}
$$

where $\hat{u}_i$ ($i = 1, 2, \ldots, n$) denotes the derivative of $u(\cdot)$ with respect to its ith argument evaluated at the point $\hat{x}$. $\hat{\lambda}$ is a nonnegative scalar Lagrange multiplier which has the (cardinal) interpretation of the current marginal utility of income when prices are evaluated at $\hat{p}$ and income is $\hat{y}$.

Next we solve for that income y that makes the individual currently indifferent between his current constraints and his base period constraints. y is defined by

$$
p'x - y = 0, \tag{3.2}
$$

where p is the column vector of current prices, $p' = (p_1, p_2, \ldots, p_n)$, where

p_i $(i = 1, 2, \ldots, n)$ is the current price of the ith good. x is the column vector of purchases, $x' = (x_1, x_2, \ldots, x_n)$, that minimizes y subject to $u(bx_1, x_2, \ldots, x_n) = u(b\hat{x}_1, \hat{x}_2, \ldots, \hat{x}_n)$. Constrained minimization of y implies that

$$
\begin{pmatrix} u \\ bu_1 \\ u_2 \\ \cdot \\ \cdot \\ \cdot \\ u_n \end{pmatrix} - \begin{pmatrix} \hat{u} \\ \text{---} \\ \lambda p \end{pmatrix} = 0 , \tag{3.3}
$$

where u_i $(i = 1, 2, \ldots, n)$ denotes differentiation of $u(\cdot)$ with respect to its ith argument evaluated at x, $\hat{u}$ denotes $u(b\hat{x}_1, \hat{x}_2, \ldots, \hat{x}_n)$, and λ is a nonnegative Lagrange multiplier.

We are interested in how the true cost-of-living index $(y/\hat{y})$ is affected by taste change. Thus, it is necessary to develop the total derivative of y with respect to b. Base-period income $\hat{y}$, base-period prices $\hat{p}$, and current prices p are the given data of the problem. We evaluate $(\partial y / \partial b)$ in steps.

Lemma 3.1. $\left(\dfrac{\partial y}{\partial b} \right)_{u = \hat{u} \text{ const.}} = \dfrac{- p_1 x_1}{b} .$

Proof. Total differentiation of (3.3) with respect to b yields:

$$
\begin{bmatrix} 0 & bu_1 & u_2 & \cdots & u_n \\ p_1 & b^2 u_{11} & bu_{12} & \cdots & bu_{1n} \\ p_2 & bu_{21} & u_{22} & \cdots & u_{2n} \\ \cdot & \cdot & \cdot & & \cdot \\ \cdot & \cdot & \cdot & & \cdot \\ \cdot & \cdot & \cdot & & \cdot \\ p_n & bu_{n1} & u_{n2} & & u_{nn} \end{bmatrix} \begin{bmatrix} -\dfrac{\partial \lambda}{\partial b} \\ \text{------} \\ \dfrac{\partial x}{\partial b} \end{bmatrix} + \begin{bmatrix} x_1 u_1 \\ u_1 + bx_1 u_{11} \\ x_1 u_{12} \\ \cdot \\ \cdot \\ \cdot \\ x_1 u_{1n} \end{bmatrix} = 0 , \tag{3.4}
$$

where u_{ij} $(i, j = 1, 2, \ldots, n)$ denotes partial differentiation of u_i with respect to its jth argument and $(\partial x / \partial b)$ denotes the column vector $(\partial x_1 / \partial b, \partial x_2 / \partial b, \ldots, \partial x_n / \partial b)'$. Denote the nonsingular $(n+1) \times (n+1)$ matrix in

(3.4) by H. Then:

$$
\begin{bmatrix}
-\dfrac{\partial \lambda}{\partial b} \\
\text{------} \\
\dfrac{\partial x}{\partial b}
\end{bmatrix}
= -H^{-1}
\begin{bmatrix}
x_1 u_1 \\
u_1 + b x_1 u_{11} \\
x_1 u_{12} \\
. \\
. \\
. \\
x_1 u_{1n}
\end{bmatrix}
. \tag{3.5}
$$

But from (3.2) and (3.3)

$$
\left(\frac{\partial y}{\partial b}\right)_{u = \hat{u} \text{ const.}}
= p' \left(\frac{\partial x}{\partial b}\right)
= (0 \mid p')
\begin{pmatrix}
-\dfrac{\partial \lambda}{\partial b} \\
\text{------} \\
\dfrac{\partial x}{\partial b}
\end{pmatrix}
$$

$$
= -(0 \mid p') H^{-1}
\begin{pmatrix}
x_1 u_1 \\
u_1 + b x_1 u_{11} \\
x_1 u_{12} \\
. \\
. \\
. \\
x_1 u_{1n}
\end{pmatrix}
\tag{3.6}
$$

in view of (3.5). By (3.3), the first row in H is equal to λ times $(0 \mid p')$ so by the definition of the matrix inverse we have that

$$
\left(\frac{\partial y}{\partial b}\right)_{u = \hat{u} \text{ const.}}
= \frac{-x_1 u_1}{\lambda} = \frac{-p_1 x_1}{b}
\tag{3.7}
$$

by (3.3), which proves the lemma.

Following the practice in capital theory, a fruitful way to understand Lemma 3.1 is to proceed by measuring the purchases of the various goods in (utility) efficiency units. Let x^*, the vector of purchases *measured in efficiency units*, be defined by

$$
x^{*\prime} = (x_1^*, x_2^*, \ldots, x_n^*) = (b x_1, x_2, \ldots, x_n) .
\tag{3.8}
$$

Since the corresponding vector of *prices per efficiency unit* is ($p_1/b, p_2, \ldots, p_n$), income y can be written as

$$y = (p_1/b, p_2, \ldots, p_n)x^* . \tag{3.9}$$

Holding x^* fixed, differentiating (3.9) with respect to b yields

$$\left(\frac{\partial y}{\partial b}\right)_{x^* \text{ const.}} = \frac{-p_1 x_1}{b} = \left(\frac{\partial y}{\partial b}\right)_{u = \hat{u} \text{ const.}} \tag{3.10}$$

by Lemma 3.1, if x^* and b are such that the system (3.3) is satisfied. Thus the effect on y along a constant utility surface of a first-order change in the taste parameter b is the same as the effect on y, holding the amount of purchases measured in efficiency units constant, of a first-order change in the taste parameter b.[12]

Now define $(\partial \hat{x}/\partial b)$ to be the column vector with ith entry $(\partial \hat{x}_i/\partial b)$ and let $(\partial \hat{u}/\partial \hat{x})$ be the column vector with ith entry $(\partial u/\partial x_i)$ evaluated at $\hat{x}$.

Lemma 3.2. $\left(\dfrac{\partial \hat{u}}{\partial \hat{x}}\right)'\left(\dfrac{\partial \hat{x}}{\partial b}\right) = 0 .$

Proof. Totally differentiating (3.1) with respect to b yields

$$\begin{bmatrix} 0 & \hat{p}_1 & \hat{p}_2 & \cdots & \hat{p}_n \\ \hat{p}_1 & b^2\hat{u}_{11} & b\hat{u}_{12} & \cdots & b\hat{u}_{1n} \\ \hat{p}_2 & b\hat{u}_{21} & \hat{u}_{22} & \cdots & \hat{u}_{2n} \\ \cdot & \cdot & \cdot & & \cdot \\ \cdot & \cdot & \cdot & & \cdot \\ \cdot & \cdot & \cdot & & \cdot \\ \hat{p}_n & b\hat{u}_{n1} & \hat{u}_{n2} & \cdots & \hat{u}_{nn} \end{bmatrix} \begin{bmatrix} -\dfrac{\partial \hat{\lambda}}{\partial b} \\ \text{------} \\ \dfrac{\partial \hat{x}}{\partial b} \end{bmatrix} +$$

$$+ \begin{bmatrix} 0 \\ \hat{u}_1 + b\hat{x}_1\hat{u}_{11} \\ \hat{x}_1\hat{u}_{12} \\ \cdot \\ \cdot \\ \cdot \\ \hat{x}_1\hat{u}_{1n} \end{bmatrix} = 0 . \tag{3.11}$$

The $\hat{u}_{ij}$ $(i,j = 1,2,\ldots,n)$ are the cross partials defined previously but evaluated at $\hat{x}$. Let $\hat{J}$ denote the nonsingular matrix in (3.11). Then from (3.1) and (3.11)

$$\left(\frac{\partial\hat{u}}{\partial\hat{x}}\right)'\left(\frac{\partial\hat{x}}{\partial b}\right) = \hat{\lambda}(0\mid\hat{p}')\begin{pmatrix}-\dfrac{\partial\lambda}{\partial b}\\ \text{-------}\\ \dfrac{\partial\hat{x}}{\partial b}\end{pmatrix}$$

$$= -\hat{\lambda}(0\mid\hat{p}')\hat{J}^{-1}\begin{pmatrix}0\\ \hat{u}_1+b\hat{x}_1\hat{u}_{11}\\ \hat{x}_1\hat{u}_{12}\\ \cdot\\ \cdot\\ \cdot\\ \hat{x}_1\hat{u}_{1n}\end{pmatrix},\qquad(3.12)$$

which equals zero because $(0\mid\hat{p}')$ is the first row in $\hat{J}$. Lemma 3.2 is an 'envelope theorem' where the change in $\hat{u}$ due to a first order change in b *ceteris paribus* is exactly equal to the change in $\hat{u}$ due to first-order change in b when $\hat{x}$ is allowed to vary optimally (*mutatis mutandis*).

Lemma 3.3. $\left(\dfrac{\partial y}{\partial\hat{u}}\right) = \dfrac{1}{\lambda} > 0$.

Lemma 3.3 taken with Lemma 3.2 has the familiar interpretation that λ is the current marginal utility of income when prices are evaluated at p and income is y.

Proof. Total differentiation of (3.2) with respect to $\hat{u}$ yields

$$H\begin{pmatrix}-\dfrac{\partial\lambda}{\partial\hat{u}}\\ \text{------}\\ \dfrac{\partial x}{\partial\hat{u}}\end{pmatrix} = \begin{pmatrix}1\\ 0\\ \cdot\\ \cdot\\ \cdot\\ 0\end{pmatrix},\qquad(3.13)$$

where $(\partial x/\partial\hat{u})$ is an n-dimensional column vector with ith entry $(\partial x_i/\partial\hat{u})$. Differentiating (3.2) with respect to $\hat{u}$ and substituting from (3.13) yields

$$\frac{\partial y}{\partial \hat{u}} = p'\left(\frac{\partial x}{\partial \hat{u}}\right) = (0 \mid p')H^{-1}\begin{pmatrix} 1 \\ 0 \\ \cdot \\ \cdot \\ \cdot \\ 0 \end{pmatrix} = \frac{1}{\lambda}, \qquad (3.14)$$

because the first row in H is equal to $\lambda(0 \mid p')$.

From (3.1)–(3.3), total differentiation of y with respect to the parameter b gives

$$\frac{\partial y}{\partial b} = \left(\frac{\partial y}{\partial b}\right)_{u=\hat{u}\text{ const.}} + \left(\frac{\partial y}{\partial \hat{u}}\right)\left[\hat{x}_1\hat{u}_1 + \left(\frac{\partial \hat{u}}{\partial \hat{x}}\right)'\left(\frac{\partial \hat{x}}{\partial b}\right)\right]. \qquad (3.15)$$

Theorem 3.1. $\dfrac{\partial y}{\partial b} = \dfrac{p_1 x_1}{b}\left(\dfrac{\hat{x}_1\hat{u}_1}{x_1 u_1} - 1\right).$

Proof. Substitute the results of Lemmas 3.1–3.3 into equation (3.15) and then simplify by using equations (3.1) and (3.3) to establish the theorem.

Substituting from (3.1) and (3.3), (3.15) can be rewritten as

$$\frac{\partial y}{\partial b} = \frac{\hat{x}_1\hat{u}_1 - x_1 u_1}{\lambda}. \qquad (3.16)$$

Notice that the numerator of the RHS of (3.16) is the *ceteris paribus* increase in current utility when facing base-period prices minus the *ceteris paribus* increase in current utility when facing current prices, due to a first order increase in the value of b. By Lemma 3.2, we recognize the numerator of the RHS of (3.16) as the additional compensation in units of utility required to keep the consumer indifferent between base period and current constraints when b changes. Since Lemma 3.3 allows λ the interpretation of the marginal utility of income, the full fraction on the RHS of (3.16) gives the same additional compensation in money units.[13]

Corollary 3.1. If $p = \hat{p}$, then $\left(\dfrac{\partial y}{\partial b}\right) = 0$.

Proof. The corollary is an immediate consequence of Theorem 3.1. The corollary is obvious from consideration of the definition of the true cost-of-living index. After all, if $p = \hat{p}$ then $y = \hat{y}$ for all values of b.

Since we know that $(\partial y/\partial b)$ is zero when current prices equal base-period prices, in order to study the effect of taste change on the true cost-of-living index it is natural to investigate the qualitative behavior of $(\partial y/\partial b)$ when prices are displaced from $\hat{p}$. In particular, we want to derive results concerning the sign of $(\partial y/\partial b)$ for values of p different from $\hat{p}$.

To do this, it is convenient to define $z(p) = x_1 u_1$ and to study the effects of price changes upon $z(p)$.

Lemma 3.4. $\dfrac{\partial u_1}{\partial p_1} = \dfrac{u_1}{\lambda} \dfrac{\partial \lambda}{\partial p_1} + \dfrac{u_1}{p_1}$, and

$$\frac{\partial u_1}{\partial p_i} = \frac{u_1}{\lambda} \frac{\partial \lambda}{\partial p_i} \text{ for } i = 2, \ldots, n.$$

Proof. From (3.3) we have that $\dfrac{\partial u_1}{\partial p_i} = \dfrac{1}{b} \dfrac{\partial(\lambda p_1)}{\partial p_i}$ for $i = 1, 2, \ldots, n$. The

lemma follows immediately.

Lemma 3.5. $\dfrac{1}{\lambda} \left(\dfrac{\partial \lambda}{\partial p_i} \right) = - \left(\dfrac{\partial x_i}{\partial y} \right)_{p \text{ const.}}$, for $i = 1, 2, \ldots, n$.

Proof. Total differentiation of (3.3) with respect to p_i yields

$$\begin{pmatrix} \dfrac{-\partial \lambda}{\partial p_i} \\ \text{-----} \\ \dfrac{\partial x}{\partial p_i} \end{pmatrix} = H^{-1} \begin{pmatrix} 0 \\ \cdot \\ \cdot \\ \cdot \\ 0 \\ \lambda \\ 0 \\ \cdot \\ \cdot \\ \cdot \\ 0 \end{pmatrix}, \tag{3.17}$$

where $\left(\dfrac{\partial x}{\partial p_i} \right)$ is a column vector with ith entry $(\partial x_i / \partial p_i)$. The column vector on the RHS of (3.17) has λ for its $(i+1)$st entry with all other entries zero. Therefore

$$\frac{1}{\lambda} \left(\frac{\partial \lambda}{\partial p_i} \right) = -(1 \ 0 \ldots 0) H^{-1} \begin{pmatrix} 0 \\ \cdot \\ \cdot \\ \cdot \\ 0 \\ 1 \\ 0 \\ \cdot \\ \cdot \\ \cdot \\ 0 \end{pmatrix}, \tag{3.18}$$

where the unit in the column vector in (3.18) appears in the $(i+1)$st entry. The LHS of (3.18) is thus shown to be equal to minus the element in the first row and $(i+1)$st column of H^{-1} which in turn is equal to minus the element in the first row and $(i+1)$st column of the matrix J^{-1} where J is defined by

$$
J = \begin{bmatrix}
0 & p_1 & p_2 & \cdots & p_n \\
p_1 & b^2 u_{11} & bu_{12} & \cdots & bu_{1n} \\
p_2 & bu_{21} & u_{22} & \cdots & u_{2n} \\
\cdot & \cdot & \cdot & & \cdot \\
\cdot & \cdot & \cdot & & \cdot \\
\cdot & \cdot & \cdot & & \cdot \\
p_n & bu_{n1} & u_{n2} & \cdots & u_{nn}
\end{bmatrix} .
$$

This follows because only the first rows of H and J differ and they only differ by a scalar multiple. Consideration of the evaluation of inverses by the adjoint method shows that except for their first entries the first rows of H^{-1} and J^{-1} must be equal. Substituting J^{-1} for H^{-1} in (3.18) and transposing both sides yields

$$
\frac{1}{\lambda}\left(\frac{\partial \lambda}{\partial p_i}\right) = -(0 \ldots 0\ 1\ 0 \ldots 0)J^{-1}\begin{pmatrix} 1 \\ 0 \\ \cdot \\ \cdot \\ \cdot \\ 0 \end{pmatrix}
\tag{3.19}
$$

because J^{-1} is a symmetric matrix.

If the first equation in the system (3.3) is replaced by equation (3.2) and the resulting system is totally differentiated with respect to y holding prices constant, then we have

$$
J\begin{pmatrix} \dfrac{-\partial \lambda}{\partial y} \\ \text{------} \\ \dfrac{\partial x}{\partial y} \end{pmatrix}_{p \text{ const.}} = \begin{pmatrix} 1 \\ 0 \\ \cdot \\ \cdot \\ \cdot \\ 0 \end{pmatrix},
\tag{3.20}
$$

where $(\partial x/\partial y)$ is a column vector with ith entry $(\partial x_i/\partial y)$. It follows immediately from (3.20) that

$$\left(\frac{\partial x_i}{\partial y}\right)_{p \text{ const.}} = (0\ldots0\ 1\ 0\ldots0)J^{-1}\begin{pmatrix} 1 \\ 0 \\ \cdot \\ \cdot \\ \cdot \\ 0 \end{pmatrix}, \qquad (3.21)$$

where the unit in the row vector on the RHS of (3.21) appears in the $(i+1)$st entry. The lemma follows after combining (3.19) and (3.21).

Next define the elasticity of demand for the ith good with respect to the first price by

$$\eta_{i1} = \left(\frac{p_1}{x_i}\right)\left(\frac{\partial x_i}{\partial p_1}\right)_{y \text{ const.}}$$

for $i = 1,2,\ldots,n$.

Lemma 3.6. If $z(p) = x_1 u_1$, then

$$\frac{\partial z}{\partial p_1} = \frac{x_1 u_1}{p_1}\{\eta_{11}+1\} \quad \text{and}$$

$$\frac{\partial z}{\partial p_i} = \frac{x_i u_1}{p_1}\eta_{i1}, \quad i = 2,\ldots,n\,.$$

Proof. By Lemmas 3.4 and 3.5

$$\frac{\partial z}{\partial p_1} = u_1\left[\left(\frac{\partial x_1}{\partial p_1}\right)_{u=\hat{u} \text{ const.}} - x_1\left(\frac{\partial x_1}{\partial y}\right)_{p \text{ const.}} + \frac{x_1}{p_1}\right] \text{and}$$

$$\frac{\partial z}{\partial p_i} = u_1\left[\left(\frac{\partial x_1}{\partial p_i}\right)_{u=\hat{u} \text{ const.}} - x_1\left(\frac{\partial x_i}{\partial y}\right)_{p \text{ const.}}\right], i = 2,\ldots,n\,. \quad (3.22)$$

Because substitution effects are symmetric, in (3.22), $(\partial x_1/\partial p_i)_{u=\hat{u} \text{ const.}}$ can be replaced by $(\partial x_i/\partial p_1)_{u=\hat{u} \text{ const.}}$. Application of Slutsky's theorem then yields

$$\frac{\partial z}{\partial p_1} = u_1\left[\left(\frac{\partial x_1}{\partial p_1}\right)_{y \text{ const.}} + \frac{x_1}{p_1}\right] \text{and}$$

$$\frac{\partial z}{\partial p_i} = u_1\left(\frac{\partial x_i}{\partial p_1}\right)_{y \text{ const.}}, i = 2,\ldots,n\,. \qquad (3.23)$$

Using the definition of the η_{i1} in (3.23) and rearranging completes the proof of the lemma.

We must now agree on some terminology. We shall call the demand for the first good *price elastic* (*price inelastic*) if $\eta_{11} < (>) - 1$. Next, we shall call the ith good a *gross substitute* (*gross complement*) for the first good if $\eta_{i1} > (<) 0$ ($i = 2, \ldots, n$). Note that this relation is not symmetric; the ith good can be a gross substitute for the first good while the first good is a gross complement for the ith good. This, of course, is due to income effects. The symmetric substitution relationships defined by the substitution terms in the Slutsky equation we shall refer to as those of *net substitutes* or *net complements*.

Theorem 3.2. (A) Suppose $p_i = \hat{p}_i$ for $i = 2, \ldots, n$. If the demand for the first good is price elastic, then $(\partial y / \partial b)$ has the same sign as $(p_1 - \hat{p}_1)$. If that demand is price inelastic, then $(\partial y / \partial b)$ and $(p_1 - \hat{p}_1)$ have opposite signs. If $\eta_{11} = -1$, then $(\partial y / \partial b) = 0$.

(B) Suppose $p_i = \hat{p}_i$ for $i = 1, \ldots, n$ and $i \neq j \neq 1$. If the jth good is a gross complement for the first good, then $(\partial y / \partial b)$ has the same sign as $(p_j - \hat{p}_j)$. If the jth good is a gross substitute for the first good, then $(\partial y / \partial b)$ and $(p_j - \hat{p}_j)$ have opposite signs. If $\eta_{j1} = 0$, then $(\partial y / \partial b) = 0$.

(C) If $p_i = k\hat{p}_i$, $i = 1, 2, \ldots, n$, where k is a positive constant, then $(\partial y / \partial b) = 0$.

Proof. (A) and (B) follow directly from Theorem 3.1, Corollary 3.1, and Lemma 3.6.

(C) Totally differentiating z with respect to k yields

$$k\frac{\partial z}{\partial k} = u_1 x_1 + u_1 \sum_1^n p_i \left(\frac{\partial x_i}{\partial p_1} \right)_{y \text{ const.}} \tag{3.24}$$

by Lemma 3.6 since $k(\partial p_i / \partial k) = p_i$ by hypothesis. But from (3.2), $\sum_1^n p_i \left(\frac{\partial x_i}{\partial p_1} \right)_{y \text{ const.}} = -x_1$. Theorem 3.2 (C) follows from Theorem 3.1 and Corollary 3.1.

Notice that Theorem 3.2 (A) is a *global* result (i.e. it is a result that holds for all values of p_1) when the sign of $(\eta_{11} + 1)$ is independent of the value of p_1. Likewise, Theorem 3.2 (B) is a global result when the sign of η_{j1} is independent of the value of p_j. Theorem 3.2 (C) is an extension of Corollary 3.1. If current prices are all k times base-period prices then the income that makes the consumer currently indifferent between current constraints and base-period constraints is equal to k times base-period income regardless of the value of b.[14]

Theorem 3.2 has important practical implications and may be interpreted as follows. Suppose first that all prices except the jth are the same in the two periods ($1 \leqslant j \leqslant n$). If tastes did not change ($b = 1$), the only change in the cost-of-living index would be due to the change in the value of the jth price from $\hat{p}_j$ to p_j and would, of course, be in the same direction. Assuming b to be increasing through time, if $(\partial y / \partial b)$ has the same sign as $(p_j - \hat{p}_j)$, the effect of the taste change is to magnify the effect of the change in p_j. One can express this by saying that the jth good ought to receive increased weight in the index because of the taste change. Similarly, if $(\partial y / \partial b)$ and $(p_j - \hat{p}_j)$ have opposite signs, the effect of the taste change reduces the effect of the change in p_j and the jth good ought to receive a decreased weight. Since we can always analyze a change in more than one price (for our purposes) as a series of individual price changes (because of the definition of the true cost-of-living index), these conclusions are not restricted to cases in which only one price changes between the two periods considered. Thus, Theorem 3.2 suggests that in practice, when computing a cost-of-living index, the recently introduced good should receive more weight (less weight) if demand for it is price elastic (price inelastic) than it would in a price index that does not allow for taste change. Similarly the prices of the goods that are gross complements for the recently introduced good should receive more weight and gross substitutes less weight than they would be given in a traditional price index.

Under certain conditions, e.g. homotheticity of the indifference map, we know that the true cost-of-living index $(y/\hat{y})$ is such that

$$\left(\frac{p'x}{\hat{p}'x}\right) \leqslant \left(\frac{y}{\hat{y}}\right) \leqslant \left(\frac{p'\hat{x}}{\hat{p}'\hat{x}}\right) \tag{3.25}$$

because the price indices on the left and the right do not account for substitution effects. The price index on the left of (3.25) is the (current weight) Paasche index. If tastes have not changed, the price index on the right is equal to the (base-period weight) Laspeyres index, since in that case the vector $\hat{x}$ is equal to the vector $\tilde{x}$, an n-dimensional column vector with ith entry $\tilde{x}_i$ denoting the quantity of the ith good actually purchased during the base period. Since the vector $\hat{x}$ is not observed while the vector $\tilde{x}$ is observed, it is of interest to know the relationship of the Laspeyres index $(p'\tilde{x}/\hat{p}'\tilde{x})$ to the unobserved index $(p'\hat{x}/\hat{p}'\hat{x})$. This is the purpose of the next theorem.

Theorem 3.3. (A) $\dfrac{\partial \hat{x}_1}{\partial b} = \dfrac{-\hat{x}_1}{b}(1+\eta_{11})$

(B) $\dfrac{\partial \hat{x}_i}{\partial b} = \dfrac{-\hat{x}_i}{b}\,\eta_{i1},\, i = 2,\ldots,n$.

Proof. Theorem 3.3 can be easily proved by appropriate manipulation of equation (3.11). It is more interesting, however, to analyze the problem when purchases are measured in efficiency units. Let $\hat{x}_1^* = b\hat{x}_1$ be the amount of the first good purchased (measured in efficiency units) when prices are $\hat{p}$. $\hat{p}_1^* = (\hat{p}_1/b)$ is the price per efficiency unit of the first good. The equilibrium amounts of purchases measured in efficiency units depend only upon prices per efficiency unit and income $\hat{y}$. For $\hat{p}_1^*$ fixed, the amounts of equilibrium purchases are independent of the values of b and $\hat{p}_1$. Therefore we conclude that

$$\left(\frac{\partial \hat{x}_1^*}{\partial b}\right)\left(\frac{\partial b}{\partial \hat{p}_1^*}\right)_{\hat{p}_1 \text{ const.}} = \left(\frac{\partial \hat{x}_1^*}{\partial \hat{p}_1}\right)\left(\frac{\partial \hat{p}_1}{\partial \hat{p}_1^*}\right)_{b \text{ const.}} \qquad (3.26)$$

and $$\left(\frac{\partial \hat{x}_i}{\partial b}\right)\left(\frac{\partial b}{\partial \hat{p}_1^*}\right)_{\hat{p}_1 \text{ const.}} = \left(\frac{\partial \hat{x}_i}{\partial \hat{p}_1}\right)\left(\frac{\partial \hat{p}_1}{\partial \hat{p}_1^*}\right)_{b \text{ const.}},\, i = 2,\ldots,n\,. \quad (3.27)$$

Using the definitions of $\hat{x}_1^*$, $\hat{p}_1^*$, and η_{11} in (3.26) yields (A). Using the definitions of p_1^* and η_{i1} in (3.27) yields (B). The price elasticities of demand $\eta_{i1},\, i = 1,2,\ldots,n$, in (A) and (B) are evaluated at $\hat{p}$, $\hat{x}$, and $\hat{y}$.

Again consider the case in which the first good has been recently introduced and thus the value of b has been increasing through time. Theorem 3.3 tells us, e.g. that if the price of the recently introduced good has fallen ($\hat{p}_1 > p_1$) and the demand for the first good is price elastic while the prices of all goods that are gross complements (gross substitutes) for the first good are falling (rising), then $(p'\tilde{x}/\hat{p}'\tilde{x}) > (p'\hat{x}/\hat{p}'\hat{x})$. In this special case, therefore, the value of the true cost-of-living index lies between the values of the Paasche and Laspeyres price indices (subject, of course, to the qualifications discussed in footnote 7). This result can also be deduced from Theorem 3.2 because in this special case $(\partial y/\partial b) < 0$.

Theorem 3.3 reinforces Theorem 3.2. It tells us that had current tastes been in force during the base period, purchases of gross complements for the recently introduced good would have been greater and purchases of gross substitutes less than was actually the case. Similarly, the demand for the good itself would have been greater (less) if its demand is price elastic.

It follows that in constructing a Laspeyres price index, the price of the recently introduced good should receive more weight (less weight) if demand for it is price elastic (price inelastic). Similarly the prices of goods that are gross complements (gross substitutes) for the recently introduced good should receive more weight (less weight). Theorem 3.2 assures us that similar weight changes should be made in a true cost-of-living index (a Paasche index, of course, needs no such corrections).[15]

We have stated Theorem 3.2 (and interpreted Theorem 3.3) in qualitative terms to give them some practical usefulness. In practice, one might very well be willing to say that a taste change of the sort described (a change in b) has occurred, but it is unlikely that one would be willing to say by how much b has changed. Obviously, if such information were somehow available, our lemmas would yield precise quantitative results.

Theorems 3.1–3.3 can be extended to include cases where more than one good has experienced an own-augmenting taste change. For example, consider the case in which the first two goods have been recently introduced so that the preference maps can be represented by the utility function $u(b_1 x_1, b_2 x_2, x_3, \ldots, x_n)$ where b_1 and b_2 have been increasing through time. In constructing a cost-of-living index, prices of those goods that are gross complements (gross substitutes) for *both* of the recently introduced goods should receive more weight (less weight). If demand for the first good is elastic and demand for the second is inelastic, if the first and second goods are gross substitutes for each other, and if $(b_1/b_2) > 1$ in the current period while $(b_1/b_2) = 1$ during the base period, then the first good should receive more weight and the second good less weight.

Before closing this section, we may briefly ask a second-order question. Do the effects described in Theorem 3.2 get larger with larger price changes or do they decrease as price changes increase? This question is of some interest if attention is to be paid to such effects in practice. Since, as in Theorem 3.2, it suffices to look at one price change at a time, we may answer it by examining $(\partial^2 y / \partial b \, \partial p_j) \ (j = 1, \ldots, n)$.

Define the *net* price elasticity of demand η^n_{j1} by

$$\eta^n_{j1} = \left(\frac{p_j}{x_1}\right)\left(\frac{\partial x_1}{\partial p_j}\right)_{u = \hat{u} \text{ const}}, \quad j = 1, \ldots, n. \tag{3.28}$$

Lemma 3.7. $\quad \dfrac{\partial^2 y}{\partial b \partial p_1} = \left(\dfrac{1}{p_1}\right)\left(\dfrac{\partial y}{\partial b}\right)\{\eta^n_{11} + 1\} - \left(\dfrac{\hat{x}_1 \hat{u}_1}{b u_1}\right)(\eta_{11} + 1)$

and
$$\frac{\partial^2 y}{\partial b \partial p_j} = \left(\frac{1}{p_j}\right)\left(\frac{\partial y}{\partial b}\right)\eta_{j1}^n - \left(\frac{\hat{x}_1 \hat{u}_1 x_j}{b x_1 u_1}\right)\eta_{j1} \ (j = 2, ..., n).$$

Proof. This follows immediately from Theorem 3.1 and Lemma 3.6.

We may now state:

Theorem 3.4. (A) Suppose that $p_i = \hat{p}_i$, $i = 2, . . ., n$. For p_1 sufficiently close to $\hat{p}_1$, $(\partial^2 y / \partial b \, \partial p_1)$ is positive if the demand for the first good is elastic and negative if it is inelastic. Further, if $\eta_{11}^n \geqslant -1$, the same statement holds for all $p_1 > \hat{p}_1$; if $\eta_{11}^n \leqslant -1$, it holds for all $p_1 < \hat{p}_1$.[16]

(B) Suppose that $p_i = \hat{p}_i$ for $i = 1, . . ., n$ and $i \neq j \neq 1$. For p_j sufficiently close to $\hat{p}_j$, $(\partial^2 y / \partial b \, \partial p_j)$ is positive if the jth good is a gross complement for the first good and negative if the jth good is a gross substitute for the first good. Further, if the two goods are *net* substitutes (or if $\eta_{j1}^n = 0$), the same statement holds for all $p_j > \hat{p}_j$; if they are *net* complements (or if $\eta_{j1}^n = 0$), it holds for all $p_j < \hat{p}_j$.

Proof. The statements about sufficiently small price changes follow from Lemma 3.7 and Corollary 3.1. The remaining statements follow from Lemma 3.7 and Theorem 3.2.

Thus, for all cases which can be definitely determined, the second-order effects being examined reinforce the first-order ones already treated. The effects of taste change on proper weights in the cost-of-living index are bigger for bigger price changes. For example, we have already seen in Theorem 3.2 that the weight given a gross complement for the first good should be increased on account of the taste change. We now see that for small changes in the price of that complement this effect gets bigger the bigger the price change, and that this remains true globally if the goods are also net complements and the price of the good in question has fallen. Similarly, if the jth good is a gross substitute for the first good, the weight given the jth good should be decreased as a result of the taste change. The amount of decrease should be greater, the higher is p_j above $\hat{p}_j$, provided that the two goods are net substitutes as well.[17]

IV. *New Goods and Other Corner Solutions*

In the previous section, we restricted our analysis of taste change to cases where the relevant maxima and minima are given by interior solutions to the first-order conditions. This section is devoted to a general analysis of the treatment of corner solutions in the cost-of-living index. The problem of this type that is most frequently encountered in practice is the problem of 'new goods'. For our purposes, a new good is one that is purchased in positive amount during the current period but for which base-period purchases were zero. The opposite case of 'disappearing goods', where purchases of the disappearing goods were positive in the base period but are zero in the current period, is also of practical interest.

Using the vector form of the notation developed in (2.1)–(2.4), the problem is to find that income y that makes the representative consumer currently indifferent between facing current prices p with income y and facing base-period prices $\hat{p}$ and base-period income $\hat{y}$. Formally the problem is to solve for a nonnegative vector of purchases x such that

$$\left(\frac{\partial u}{\partial x}\right) - \lambda p \leqslant 0 , \tag{4.1}$$

where $(\partial u / \partial x)$ is a column vector with ith entry $(\partial u / \partial x_i)$, $i = 1, 2, \ldots, n$,

$$x' \left[\left(\frac{\partial u}{\partial x}\right) - \lambda p\right] = 0 , \tag{4.2}$$

$$x \geqslant 0 \quad \text{and} \quad \lambda \geqslant 0 . \tag{4.3}$$

x is constrained by $u(x) = u(\hat{x})$ or simply

$$u - \hat{u} = 0 , \tag{4.4}$$

where $\hat{x}$ solves the system

$$\left(\frac{\partial \hat{u}}{\partial \hat{x}}\right) - \hat{\lambda} \hat{p} \leqslant 0 , \tag{4.5}$$

where $(\partial \hat{u} / \partial \hat{x})$ denotes the vector $(\partial u / \partial x)$ evaluated at $\hat{x}$,

$$\hat{x}' \left[\left(\frac{\partial \hat{u}}{\partial \hat{x}}\right) - \hat{\lambda} \hat{p}\right] = 0 , \tag{4.6}$$

$$\hat{\lambda}(\hat{y} - \hat{p}' \hat{x}) = 0, \tag{4.7}$$

$$\hat{x} \geqslant 0 \quad \text{and} \quad \hat{\lambda} \geqslant 0 . \tag{4.8}$$

Income y is defined by

$$y - p'x = 0 , \tag{4.9}$$

and $(y / \hat{y})$ is the true cost-of-living index.[18]

Inequation (4.1) and equation (4.2) imply that if for any $k = 1, 2, \ldots, n$, $(\partial u / \partial x_k) < \lambda p_k$, then $x_k = 0$. A similar implication is drawn from (4.5) and (4.6). λ and $\hat{\lambda}$ are scalar Lagrange multipliers. In (4.7), if we assume nonsatiation in consumption then the budget constraint holds with equality.

Now assume that the kth good is a new good; that is, $x_k > 0$ with $(\partial u / \partial x_k) = \lambda p_k$ and $\tilde{x}_k = 0$, where $\tilde{x}_k$ is the *actual* amount of the kth good that was purchased during the base period. If tastes have not changed, then $\hat{x}_k = \tilde{x}_k = 0$. The difficulty in this case is that there is no recorded base-period market price for the kth good. In the case of no taste change, the computation of the true cost-of-living index which allows for corner solutions is straightforward. If, for example, the kth good is a new good, the restriction $\hat{x}_k = 0$ is added to the system (4.1)–(4.9) leaving the value of $\hat{p}_k$ as an unknown to be determined in solving the new system. Or equivalently, the system (4.1)–(4.9) is solved for y after assigning to $\hat{p}_k$ any value greater than or equal to the demand reservation price (the lowest price at which demand for the kth good is zero) including the supply reservation price (the highest price at which supply of the kth good is zero) which in some sense is the price that consumers actually faced during the base period.

Note, however, that in the base-period constrained utility maximization problem, the demand reservation price itself is the maximizing value of the shadow multiplier associated with the constraint $\hat{x}_k = 0$, since by definition the demand reservation price is what the representative consumer is willing to pay per unit (locally) for a relaxation of the constraint $\hat{x}_k = 0$.[19]

As stated in section II, it is a well-known proposition in the traditional theory of index numbers (v. Hofsten, 1952, pp. 28–9) (where it is assumed that tastes and qualities are unchanging and that all goods are purchased in positive amounts) that under certain conditions the Laspeyres (base-period weighted) price index $(p'\hat{x}/\hat{p}'\hat{x})$ bounds the true cost-of-living index from above, while the Paasche (current-period weighted) price index $(p'x/\hat{p}'x)$ bounds the true cost-of-living index from below. In the case with new goods, it is obvious that the Laspeyres index bounds the true index from above and is independent of the assignment of base-period price weights to the new goods. If we allow for the complication of new goods, however, the Paasche price index is a lower bound upon the true cost-of-living index only if we assign to the new goods, base-period prices greater than or equal to the demand reservation prices. Note, however, that of all such Paasche indices the largest (and therefore in a sense the greatest lower bound on the true cost-of-living index) is the index in which new goods purchases are weighted by their demand reservation prices. (The analysis for disappearing goods is similar and is left to the reader.)

Thus, if they are known, it is the demand reservation prices themselves which should be used to weight new-goods purchases in the construction of a Paasche index and not simply some arbitrary prices equal to or greater than the demand reservation prices. In particular, *supply* reservation prices are not relevant if the demand reservation prices are known.

This is a natural result if we recall that the demand reservation price measures (locally) the value to the base-period consumer of the relaxation of the constraint stating that the good in question is unavailable. It is the shadow price of that constraint. It is thus the demand reservation price which affects how much income the consumer would be willing to give up to relax that constraint. How much income he would in fact be techno-logically required to give up to accomplish such relaxation (the supply reservation price) is not directly germane to a theory which runs in terms of indifferent positions. If the demand reservation price is known, the supply reservation price is not relevant.

There remains the difficult practical question as to how one knows the values of demand reservation prices. To ascertain them in general might require a rather detailed demand analysis which might not be available. There are some special circumstances, however, in which demand reserva-tion prices may be less difficult to determine. Suppose that it was known that during a period for which closely spaced, time-series data are available the supply reservation price of a certain good is falling. With constant tastes and qualities and all other prices constant, the price at which the good was first marketed would then be the demand reservation price. Also, since the supply reservation price is never less than the demand reservation price, supply reservation prices can be used for new goods in the Paasche index and the latter will retain its property as lower bound on the true index (but see footnote 7).

In order to study the effects of new goods on the true cost-of-living index when tastes are changing, the previous analysis can be combined with the analysis of section III. If, for example, the first good is a new good that has experienced a positive own-augmenting taste change, if the price of the first good has fallen while all other prices have remained constant, and if demand for the first good is elastic, then by Theorems 3.2 and 3.3 the value of the true cost-of-living index is below the value of the Laspeyres index for whatever base-period prices are assigned to the new good. The Paasche index is known to be a lower bound for the true cost-of-living index if and only if the new good is assigned a base-period price greater than or equal to its demand reservation price (subject to the qualification discussed in footnote 8).

v. *Quality Change*

In this section, we take up the problem of quality change.[20] In practice, quality change is handled in the consumer price index (when it is handled at all) by assuming that an improvement in quality in a given good is equivalent to a price reduction in that good. For some cases of quality change, this is obviously the appropriate general treatment. If widgets are sold by the box and twenty widgets now are packed into the same size box as previously held ten, it is clear that this is equivalent to a halving of the price of widgets. Somewhat more generally, if one new widget delivers the same services as two old ones, this may also be considered to be simply a repackaging of widgets and thus equivalent to a price reduction.

Quality change may take other forms than that of simply augmenting the services of just that good whose quality has changed, however, and a simple adjustment of the price of that good may not suffice to account for that quality change in a cost-of-living index. Indeed, we show that such a price adjustment made independently of the amount of all goods purchased is an appropriate one if *and only if* the only effect of quality change is of the good-augmenting type just considered. Then and only then can quality change be considered a simple repackaging of the good in question.

Furthermore, while an adjustment in the price of the quality-changing good can always be made to suffice *locally* (that is, for given purchases of all goods), in general, the price adjustment which must be made will depend on all prices and purchases of all commodities and not simply on the physical characteristics of the quality change. If the new and the old qualities of the good sell in positive amount on the same (perfect) market, then all the information needed to make the appropriate *local* price adjustment for the quality change is of course coded in the difference in the prices of the two varieties. The extension of the same price adjustment to other (perhaps later) situations, however, when other prices change or other related qualities are introduced is appropriate, as stated, only in the pure repackaging case. If the two varieties do not coexist in the same (perfect) market, then even such a local price adjustment must be made to depend explicitly on the quantities of all goods purchased and not simply on physical characteristics, save in the pure repackaging case.[21]

In circumstances other than the simple repackaging case, then, we show that the simplest adjustment of the cost-of-living index may be an adjustment in the price of one or more goods *other than the one whose quality has changed*. While part of the effects of any quality change may well be to augment the services of the quality-changing good, there are likely to be other effects as well and here more than one price change is required.

Thus, for example, suppose that there is a quality change in refrigerators. If this change simply makes one new refrigerator deliver the services of some larger number of old ones, then the simplest price adjustment in the cost-of-living index is indeed an adjustment in the price of refrigerators. On the other hand, if that quality change also increases the enjoyment obtained from a quart of ice cream, then an adjustment in refrigerator price will not suffice; an adjustment in the price of ice cream is also called for. Indeed, if the *only* effect of a refrigerator quality change is to augment the enjoyment obtained from ice cream, then the simplest adjustment is one made *only* in the price of ice cream, even though the quality change takes place in refrigerators. In this case, an adjustment in the price of refrigerators can be made to suffice; the magnitude of that adjustment, however, will depend on the quantities demanded of all goods. An adjustment in the price of ice cream will also suffice; the magnitude of that adjustment, however, will only depend on the quantity of ice cream and the quantity of refrigerators.

Now, of course, this is fairly easy to see in the case of this example. Refrigerators are not directly consumed, rather, they are used as an intermediate good in the production of certain consumption goods, including cold ice cream. Thus, one can argue, since refrigerator services do not enter the utility function directly, the cost of using refrigerator services is but part of the price of the foodstuffs concerned and an improvement in refrigerator quality ought clearly to be accounted for in the prices of just those particular foodstuffs affected. If that quality improvement only changes ice cream enjoyment, then the true quality improvement is in refrigerated ice cream. An adjustment in the price of refrigerated ice cream, however, is most easily done by adjusting the price of ice cream (assuming all ice cream to be refrigerated); an adjustment in the price of refrigerators, on the other hand, affects the cost of consuming other refrigerated foodstuffs as well. Thus, in this simple example, adjustment of the price of ice cream can be made much more simply than adjustment of the price of refrigerators to achieve the same result in the cost-of-living index.

In fact, this is quite a good way to look at the matter and at our results even if refrigerator services do appear in the utility function directly, as is the case in some treatments [22] and as would certainly be the analogous case in treatments of other examples. In this case, refrigerators should *still* be looked on as an intermediate good, affecting the enjoyment of foodstuffs and also the enjoyment of its own services. As before, it is those 'final' goods whose enjoyment is affected by the quality change whose prices should be adjusted to obtain the simplest equivalent change in the cost-of-living index. The fact that one of those 'final' goods happens to have the same name and to be consumed in fixed proportions with the intermediate good does not change this statement. If this is borne in mind throughout, the interpretation of our results will be relatively straightforward.

We now turn to the formal analysis of the problem. The current (twice differentiable) utility function is given by

$$u = u(x_1, \ldots, x_n, b) \equiv u(x, b), \tag{5.1}$$

where b is a parameter measuring quality change in the first good, with $b = 1$ being the case of no quality change.[23] As quality change is to take place in the first good, it is natural to assume

$$u_b(0, x_2, \ldots, x_n, b) \equiv 0, \tag{5.2}$$

where the subscript denotes differentiation with respect to b. However, we shall not make direct use of this property.[24]

As before, in the base period, the consumer has income $\hat{y}$ and faces prices $\hat{p}$. He is also constrained in that period by only being able to purchase a quality of the first commodity for which $b = 1$. The purchases which are made under these conditions are $\hat{x}$, and the corresponding utility level is

$$\hat{u} = u(\hat{x}, 1). \tag{5.3}$$

The constraints of the present period are defined by some $b \neq 1$ and prices p. The income at which the consumer would be just indifferent between the two sets of constraints is y, and the true cost-of-living index is $y/\hat{y}$. y is thus defined as

$$y = p'x\,, \tag{5.4}$$

where x is given as the solution to the problem

$$\text{Minimize } y \text{ subject to } u(x,b) = \hat{u}\,. \tag{5.5}$$

x thus satisfies:

$$u(x,b) - \hat{u} = 0 \tag{5.6}$$

$$u_i - \lambda p_i = 0 \qquad (i = 1,\ldots,n)\,,$$

where λ is a Lagrange multiplier and is the marginal utility of income.[26]

Given $\hat{p}$ and $\hat{y}$, therefore, y is a function of p and b, and we may write

$$y = y(p,b)\,. \tag{5.7}$$

Suppose now that we wish to take account of the quality change by a suitable change in the price of the first good. We thus seek a p_1^*, such that

$$y(p_1^*,p_2,\ldots,p_n,1) = y(p_1,\ldots,p_n,b)\,. \tag{5.8}$$

For $b = 1$, $p_1^* = p_1$. As b changes from unity, p_1^* will change. Differentiating (5.8) totally with respect to b and rearranging, we have:

$$\frac{\partial p_1^*}{\partial b} = \frac{\partial y/\partial b}{\partial y/\partial p_1^*}\,. \tag{5.9}$$

We must therefore investigate $\partial y/\partial b$ and $\partial y/\partial p_1^*$.

Lemma 5.1. $\partial y/\partial b = -u_b/\lambda$.

Proof. Differentiate (5.6) totally with respect to b, obtaining

$$\begin{bmatrix} 0 & u_1 & \cdots & u_n \\ p_1 & u_{11} & \cdots & u_{1n} \\ \cdot & & & \cdot \\ \cdot & & & \cdot \\ \cdot & & & \cdot \\ p_n & u_{n1} & \cdots & u_{nn} \end{bmatrix} \begin{bmatrix} -\partial\lambda/\partial b \\ \text{-----------} \\ \partial x/\partial b \\ \cdot \\ \cdot \\ \cdot \end{bmatrix} = - \begin{bmatrix} u_b \\ u_{1b} \\ \cdot \\ \cdot \\ \cdot \\ u_{nb} \end{bmatrix}, \tag{5.10}$$

where $\partial x/\partial b$ is an n-component vector whose ith element is $\partial x_i/\partial b$.

Denote the first matrix on the left by D. Then

$$
\begin{bmatrix} -\partial\lambda/\partial b \\ \hline \partial x/\partial b \end{bmatrix} = -D^{-1} \begin{bmatrix} u_b \\ u_{1b} \\ . \\ . \\ . \\ u_{nb} \end{bmatrix}. \tag{5.11}
$$

Now,

$$
\partial y/\partial b = p'(\partial x/\partial b) = (0 \mid p') \begin{pmatrix} -\partial\lambda/\partial b \\ \hline \partial x/\partial b \end{pmatrix}
$$

$$
= \frac{1}{\lambda}(0, u_1, \ldots, u_n) \begin{pmatrix} -\partial\lambda/\partial b \\ \hline \partial x/\partial b \end{pmatrix} \tag{5.12}
$$

in view of (5.6).

However, $(0, u_1, \ldots, u_n)$ is the first row of D and the lemma now follows immediately from (5.11) and (5.12).[26]

Lemma 5.2. $\partial y/\partial p_1 = x_1$.

Proof. Differentiate (5.6) totally with respect to p_1, obtaining:

$$
\begin{pmatrix} -\partial\lambda/\partial p_1 \\ \hline \partial x/\partial p_1 \end{pmatrix} = D^{-1} \begin{bmatrix} 0 \\ \lambda \\ 0 \\ . \\ . \\ . \\ 0 \end{bmatrix}, \tag{5.13}
$$

where $\partial x/\partial p_1$ is the n-component vector whose ith element is $\partial x_i/\partial p_1$.

$$
\partial y/\partial p_1 = x_1 + p'(\partial x/\partial p_1) = x_1 + \frac{1}{\lambda}(0, u_1, \ldots, u_n) \begin{pmatrix} -\partial\lambda/\partial b \\ \hline \partial x/\partial b \end{pmatrix}. \tag{5.14}
$$

The lemma now follows as before, since $(0, u_1, \ldots, u_n)$ is the first row of D.

Thus, $\partial y/\partial p_1 = x_1$. Similarly, if we substitute p_1^* for p_1 and write x_1^* for the corresponding amount of the first commodity purchased, $\partial y/\partial p_1^* = x_1^*$. It is thus clear that as long as $x_1^* \neq 0$, p_1^* is a uniquely defined function of

b (given the other elements of p). Since at $b = 1$, $p_1^* = p_1$ no matter what the values of the other elements of p and the elements of x are, p_1^* will be independent of any subset of those elements if and only if $\partial p_1^* / \partial b$ is so independent. We therefore concentrate on the latter quantity. To avoid a burdensome notation, we always take that derivative at $b = 1$; only notational changes would be required to perform the analysis at an arbitrary b.

Combining Lemmas 5.1 and 5.2 with (5.9) and evaluating at $b = 1$, we have

Lemma 5.3. $\dfrac{\partial p_1^*}{\partial b} = \dfrac{-p_1 u_b}{x_1 u_1}$.

Proof. This follows immediately from the two preceding lemmas and (5.6).

Thus we have evaluated the adjustment which must be made in p_1 to give a result equivalent to the quality change involved in a change in b. Clearly, such an adjustment can be made (as long as $x_1 \neq 0$). That adjustment depends in general, however, on all the elements of x. Thus, in the general case, the adjustment cannot be made independent of knowledge of all purchases and the way they affect (u_b / u_1).[27] It is natural to ask under what circumstances the adjustment can be made without such knowledge or, equivalently, under what circumstances an adjustment made from market data in a given situation will retain validity when that situation changes.

Theorem 5.1. (A) A necessary and sufficient condition for $\partial p_1^* / \partial b$ to be independent of $x_2, \ldots, x_n$ is that it be possible to write the utility function in the form

$$u(x,b) = F(g(x_1,b),x_2,\ldots,x_n) \equiv F(g^*(x_1,b)x_1,x_2,\ldots,x_n)$$
$$(5.15)$$

for some choice of continuously differentiable functions F and g.[28] We write $g(x_1,b) \equiv g^*(x_1,b)x_1$ for ease of interpretation.

(B) A necessary and sufficient condition for $\partial p_1^* / \partial b$ to be independent of *all* the elements of x (including x_1) is that (5.15) hold with g in the form

$$g(x_1,b) = x_1 h(b) \quad \text{or} \quad g^*(x_1,b) = h(b) \qquad (5.16)$$

for some choice of the function h. (This is the pure repackaging case.)
Proof. (A) By Lemma 5.3, a necessary and sufficient condition for $\partial p_1^* / \partial b$

to be independent of $x_2, \ldots, x_n$, is that u_b/u_1 be so independent. This is equivalent to (5.15) by a well-known theorem of Leontief (1947a, p. 364; 1947b).

(B) In view of Lemma 5.3 and (A), a necessary and sufficient condition for $\partial p_1^*/\partial b$ to be independent of all the elements of x is that (5.15) hold and that, in addition, $\dfrac{u_b}{x_1 u_1}$ be independent of x_1. This means that it is necessary and sufficient that there exist a function $\phi(b)$ such that

$$\frac{g_b}{g_1} = \frac{u_b}{u_1} = -x_1\phi(b). \tag{5.17}$$

Now consider a curve in the $x_1 - b$ plane along which g is constant–an indifference curve of g. This is defined by

$$g(x_1,b) = \bar{g} . \tag{5.18}$$

Differentiating (5.18) totally with respect to b and rearranging:

$$dx_1/db = -\frac{g_b}{g_1} = x_1\phi(b) \tag{5.19}$$

along that curve. Thus:

$$d \log x_1 = \phi(b)\, db . \tag{5.20}$$

Integrating:

$$\log x_1 = \log \mu(b) + \log c , \tag{5.21}$$

where $\mu(b)$ is an integral of $\phi(b)$, and c is an arbitrary constant. In other words:

$$\frac{x_1}{\mu(b)} = c \tag{5.22}$$

is the equation of the indifference curve defined in (5.18).

Now, we can clearly replace g in (5.15) by any monotonic transformation of $\bar{g}$, adjusting the result by redefining F. Thus we can choose the scale on which g is measured and can do so in such a way as to make $\bar{g} = c$ without changing anything else. If we do this, however, the theorem follows immediately from (5.18) and (5.22), with $h(b) = 1/\mu(b)$.

Some remarks on the theorem are now in order.

First, as observed, part (B) of the theorem is the repackaging case. In this case, it might appear more natural to have b appearing in place of $h(b)$. $h(b)$ appears because the scaling of b is arbitrary. There is no reason not to measure quality change in this case in units of h rather than in units of b, in which case the more natural-appearing result is obtained.

Second, part (B) shows that the repackaging case is the *only* case in which the quality change is equivalent to a *simple* adjustment in the price of the first commodity. Any other case requires knowledge of the elements of x. Another way of putting this is to say that in any other case the adjustment in p_1 will be different at different points in the commodity space.

Third, part (A) shows that, even if we are willing to let the adjustment in p_1 depend on the quantity of the first good purchased, the class of quality changes in the first good which can be so handled is not really much widened. The only generalization is, in effect, to move to a sort of variable repackaging in which the amount of repackaging is allowed to depend on x_1. As soon as a quality change in the first commodity enters in a more general way–for example, by affecting other commodities–an equivalent adjustment in p_1 depends on other elements of x.[29]

Finally, if the conditions of part (A) hold, the dependence of the adjustment on the level of p_1 is of a very simple kind, given x_1. The *percentage* adjustment in p_1 which must be made is dependent only on x_1 in this case, since, given x_1, p_1 enters only multiplicatively in $\partial p_1^* / \partial b$. A similar remark applies to all later results in this section.

Theorem 5.1 can be generalized to give the conditions under which quality change is equivalent to an adjustment in p_1 which depends only on selected elements of x. Thus

Theorem 5.2. (A) For any $m = 1, \ldots, n-1$, a necessary and sufficient condition for $\partial p_1^* / \partial b$ to be independent of $x_{m+1}, \ldots, x_n$, is that it be possible to write the utility function in the form:

$$u(x,b) = F(g(x_1, \ldots, x_m, b), x_2, \ldots, x_n)$$
$$\equiv F(g^*(x_1, \ldots, x_m, b)x_1, x_2, \ldots, x_n) \tag{5.23}$$

for some choice of continuously differentiable functions F and g.[30]

(B) For any $m = 1, \ldots, n-1$, a necessary and sufficient condition for $\partial p_1^* / \partial b$ to be independent of x_1 and $x_{m+1}, \ldots, x_n$ is that (5.23) hold with g in the form

$$g(x_1, \ldots, x_m, b) = x_1 h(x_2, \ldots, x_m, b)$$
or $$g^*(x_1, \ldots, x_m, b) = h(x_2, \ldots, x_m, b), \tag{5.24}$$

for some choice of a function h.

Proof. The proof of part (A) follows again from Leontief's theorem. That of part (B) is the same as that given for part (B) of Theorem 5.1, save that the indifference variety of g is taken at fixed values of $x_2, \ldots, x_m$. The values of $x_2, \ldots, x_m$ then become parameters of $\mu(b)$.

Unfortunately, while this generalization allows us to handle a wider variety of quality change than that covered in Theorem 5.1, it still leaves us in the case of repackaging of the first commodity (although the extent of repackaging is now allowed to depend on the quantities of other commodities). It does not touch the case in which a quality change in the first commodity affects other commodities by augmenting their services, for example, the case of refrigerators and ice cream mentioned above being a case in point. This leads us to abandon the notion that simple adjustments in the price of the good whose quality has changed are likely to be generally effective and to ask whether for some quality changes adjustments in *other* prices might not be more appropriate.

Accordingly, we next examine an extreme case in which only an adjustment in the price of the second commodity is called for. There is an asymmetry in the problem. It was reasonable to ask under what conditions an adjustment in p_1 can be made independent of x_2; it is not reasonable to ask under what conditions an adjustment in p_2 can be made independent of x_1. The quality change is embodied in the first commodity and the consumer cannot take advantage of it without purchasing that commodity (see (5.2), for example). It is reasonable to ask under what circumstances an adjustment in p_2 can be made independent of the other elements of x, however, and this we shall do.

We thus replace (5.8) by

$$y(p_1, p_2^*, p_3, \ldots, p_n, 1) = y(p_1, \ldots, p_n, b).$$ (5.25)

It is clear that the argument leading to Lemma 5.3 shows

Lemma 5.4. $\dfrac{\partial p_2^*}{\partial b} = \dfrac{-p_2 u_b}{x_2 u_2}$.

We have immediately:

Theorem 5.3. (A) A necessary and sufficient condition for $\partial p_2^* / \partial b$ to be independent of $x_3, \ldots, x_n$ is that it be possible to write the utility function in the form

$$u(x,b) = F(x_1, g(x_1, x_2, b), x_3, \ldots, x_n)$$
$$\equiv F(x_1, g^*(x_1, x_2, b) x_2, x_3, \ldots, x_n)$$ (5.26)

for some choice of continuously differentiable functions F and g.[31]

(B) A necessary and sufficient condition for $\partial p_2^* / \partial b$ to be independent of $x_3, \ldots, x_n$ and x_2 is that (5.26) hold, with g in the form

$$g(x_1, x_2, b) = x_2 h(x_1, b) \quad \text{or} \quad g^*(x_1, x_2, b) = h(x_1, b) \qquad (5.27)$$

for some choice of a function h.

Proof. (A) follows from Lemma 5.4 and Leontief's theorem. (B) is proved as before, noting that x_1 is a parameter of the appropriate indifference curve of g in the $x_2 - b$ plane.

This is an interesting case. Whereas what was interesting about Theorem 5.1 was the necessity of the conditions, what is interesting here is sufficiency. Looked at in this way, the theorem tells us that if quality change in good one augments the services of good *two*, then a simple adjustment in the price of the latter good is called for. Once again, an adjustment can be made in this case in the price of good one, but Theorem 5.1 assures us that the adjustment will not be a simple one; it will depend on all commodity purchases. The simple adjustment is one in the price of the second good which is not the good whose quality has changed. If the only effect of a quality change in refrigerators is to make ice cream taste better, the simple adjustment which should be made is in the price of ice cream, not the price of refrigerators. The magnitude of that adjustment will depend on the quantity of refrigerators, and it may also depend on the quantity of ice cream (which is reasonable when one supposes that the effect depends on the ice cream–refrigerator ratio), but, unlike an adjustment in the price of refrigerators, it does not depend on the quantities of other goods.

Such polar cases, however, are too simple. In practice, quality change, even if it takes the relatively simple form of augmenting the services of certain goods, is unlikely merely to augment the services of only one good. A better refrigerator affects goods other than ice cream. Clearly, from Theorem 5.1 and 5.3, a simple adjustment in a single price will not suffice in such circumstances.

Fortunately, however, simple adjustments in more than one price will suffice, and this can be done by using our results simultaneously for more than one good. Thus, suppose that the utility function can be written in the form

$$u(x, b) = F(g^1(x_1, b), g^2(x_1, x_2, b), \ldots, g^n(x_1, x_n, b)) \qquad (5.28)$$
$$\equiv F(g^{*1}(x_1, b) x_1, g^{*2}(x_1, x_2, b) x_2, \ldots, g^{*n}(x_1, x_n, b) x_n)$$

for some choice of continuously differentiable functions, F and $g^1, \ldots, g^n$. This is the case in which every good is augmented, but, if $g^1(x_1, x_i, b) = x_i$ $(g^{*i}(x_1, x_i, b) = 1)$ for all b, then the augmentation of the ith good is zero (and similarly for the first good). This case contains all those turned up in Theorems 5.1 and 5.3; generalization along the lines of Theorem 5.2 is left to the reader.[32]

Since g^1 is to reflect the augmentation of the first commodity itself, it is obviously reasonable to assume that $g_1^1 \neq 0$.[33] Actually, we need only assume that x_1 is uniquely determined given b and g^1, i.e. that there exists a function ϕ, such that

$$x_1 = \phi(g^1(x_1, b), b) . \tag{5.29}$$

With this assumption, our previous results enable us to handle this relatively general case.

Theorem 5.4. If quality change satisfies (5.28) and (5.29), its effect on the true cost-of-living index can be equivalently represented as a set of price adjustments. The percentage adjustment in the first price depends at most on the amount of the first commodity; the percentage adjustment in the ith price $(i = 2, \ldots, n)$ depends at most on the amount of the first and ith commodities.[34]

Proof. In view of (5.29), every $g^i (i = 2, \ldots, n)$ can be written as a function of g^1, x_i, and b. Thus:

$$g^i(x_1, x_i, b) = h^i(g^1, x_i, b) \quad (i = 2, \ldots, n) . \tag{5.30}$$

We shall break up the effect of a change in b into its effects on the various commodities, as follows. Let the b appearing as an argument of g^1 be denoted b_1; let the b appearing as an argument of h^i be denoted b_i $(i = 2, \ldots, n)$. We shall begin with all the b_i equal to unity and shall change them to their common post-quality-change value, denoted $\bar{b}$, one at a time.

Thus, set all the $b_i = 1$, save b_1 and consider the effect of changing b_1 from unity to $\bar{b}$. By (5.30), b_1 enters the utility function only through g^1, and hence the condition of (A) of Theorem 5.1 is satisfied. It follows that the effect of b_1 on y can be equivalently represented as an adjustment in p_1. That adjustment (in percentage terms) depends only on x_1 and not on the other elements of x. Further, in view of Lemma 5.3, that adjustment does not depend on the values of the b_i $(i = 2, \ldots, n)$, so there is no need to remake it when we change those values.

Now move b_2 from unity to $\bar{b}$, keeping $b_1 = \bar{b}$ and $b_i = 1$ ($i = 3, \ldots, n$). With b_1 fixed, g^1 depends only on x_1, so that h^2 depends only on x_1, x_2, and b_2. It is clear that the condition of (A) of Theorem 5.3 is satisfied, so that the effect of the change in b_2 can be equivalently represented as an adjustment in p_2. That adjustment (in percentage terms) depends at most on x_1 and x_2, and, as before, is independent of the values of the b_i ($i = 3, \ldots, n$).

Next, move b_3 and adjust p_3. This adjustment is independent of the other b_i ($i = 4, \ldots, n$) and also independent of b_2. Proceeding in this way, we account for all effects of the quality change and the theorem is proved.

Thus any quality change in the first good, every effect of which can be represented as an augmentation of the services of some good[35] can be handled by adjusting in the cost-of-living index the prices of every good whose services are so augmented and *only* the prices of those goods. In the simplest case of this, given in (5.28), those adjustments (taken in percentage terms) depend at most on the quality of the first good purchased, and possibly on the purchased quantity of the good in question. These price adjustments can be made independently. More complicated cases along the lines of Theorem 5.2 can also be handled. Save in the very simplest of all cases, where only the first good itself is augmented, will a change in the price of the good whose quality has changed be sufficient. (Even then, unless the augmentation is constant, the price change will depend on the quantity of the first good that is purchased.) An adequate treatment of quality change in cost-of-living indices must pay attention to cross-good effects.[36]

FOOTNOTES FOR ESSAY I

[1] An exception is the theory of hedonic price indices where a quality change is regarded as providing a new bundle of old underlying attributes. See Court (1939), Griliches (1961, pp. 173–96), Lancaster (1966), and Stone (1956).

[2] Intertemporal comparisons which do not involve the same set of consumers at both times or geographical comparisons also sharply point up the problem. Following this testament to our ordinalist purity, it is only fair to remark that if the results of our work are to shed light on the construction of a cost-of-living index for a society or even a class within that society the existence of a 'representative consumer' must be assumed. In general, to draw welfare conclusions from aggregate price and quantity data requires interpersonal utility comparisons. For a full discussion of this point, see Samuelson (1947).

[3] Yet this is not inevitable. One can ask how the cost of living in the United Kingdom changed as seen with American tastes or how a man of today would view nineteenth-century price changes.

[4] As already observed, there is a further set of questions in which the tastes are neither those of today nor those of yesterday but are those of a wholly different third situation. For some purposes, these are quite interesting questions to ask, but we shall have nothing to say about them directly in this paper. When the indifference map used in the comparison is one not tied to the situations to be compared, then, of course, we are in the situation envisaged in existing theoretical treatments.

[5] In the case of international or interregional comparisons, both questions have equal interest. The fact that the answers may be quite different is then an inevitable consequence of the fact that people differ. The answer to the question: 'How much income would just make an American with income 100 willing to face British prices?' is not the same as that to the question: 'How much income would make an Englishman indifferent between continuing to face British prices and facing American prices with an income of 100?' Both questions are equally interesting, but they are obviously different. There *is* generally no one answer to both questions and no point in attempting to construct a single index which answers both. One way of looking at the analysis of the next section is as a demonstration of the way in which the answers to the two questions are related if British and American tastes differ in the particular way parametrized in that section.

[6] Note, however, that a policy choice made at the start of the process which did not foresee the taste changes would opt for path B. This is very similar to the myopia problem considered by Strotz (1955–6).

[7] In fact, this proposition is not true if price and income changes are large. This is because of yet another ambiguity in comparing today and yesterday that we have not discussed. The theory of the true cost-of-living index compares the expenditures required yesterday and today to reach a particular indifference curve on a stated indifference

map. But *which* indifference curve is to be used? The natural choices are the indifference curve tangent to yesterday's budget constraint and that tangent to today's. If the indifference map is not homothetic, however, a true cost-of-living index based on the first of these curves (Index A) will not generally coincide with that based on the second (Index B). Yet a moment's consideration reveals that it is Index A which is bounded from above by a Laspeyres index and Index B which is bounded from below by a Paasche index. Unless either the indifference map is homothetic (or obeys other special conditions) or price and income changes are sufficiently small to make Indices A and B close together, there is no reason why the Laspeyres index must lie above Index B or the Paasche index below Index A. Further, both A and B are equally valid and interesting indices.

In this paper, we have, for convenience, concentrated on Index A, that corresponding to the indifference curve tangent to yesterday's budget constraint. Most of our results are equally applicable to Index B, that corresponding to the indifference curve tangent to today's budget constraint. When reading statements about the bounds set by Paasche and Laspeyres indices, however, the discussion of this footnote should be kept in mind. The text implicitly includes the assumption that Index A and Index B do in fact coincide, and we have proceeded on the assumption that in fact the index under discussion is known to be bounded by the Paasche and Laspeyres indices for the case of no taste change. Without that assumption, statements about such bounds apply as statements about the relationship of the bounding index (Laspeyres or Paasche) to the appropriate true cost-of-living index (A or B). We have tried not to overburden the exposition by being explicit about this save in this footnote.

For a discussion of the problems just discussed see v. Hofsten (1952, pp. 28–9) or Malmquist (1953, pp. 221–3).

[8] Note that the implication is not that the true index lies closer to a Paasche index than to a Laspeyres. One does not know this. What one does know is that the Paasche puts a lower bound on changes in the true index, while a Laspeyres fails to have a known relation to it.

The asymmetry between Paasche and Laspeyres indices when tastes change is observed by Malmquist (1953, p. 211).

[9] We treat this case as being the simplest one to analyze. Further, the particular parametrization used not only appears in the theory of technological change but also reappears in the analysis of quality change given below as a result rather than an assumption. Of course, the present section is largely meant as an example of what can be done if an explicit model of taste change is adopted. The necessity for further work is obvious.

[10] Such cases as these may be somewhat more general than the sort of learning effect example given above and continued below. Thus, suppose that the first and second commodities in some sense serve the same needs, so that the utility function can be written as $v(g(bx_1,x_2), x_3, \ldots, x_n)$. Then a change in b might be interpreted as a change in the relative efficiency of the first two commodities in serving those needs, as perceived by the consumer. (Of course, the special form of the utility function in this case has implications for the true cost-of-living index beyond those developed below for the more general case considered in the text.) $u(\cdot)$ serves as a utility function for current *and* base-period tastes. If taste change is solely first good augmenting then the units of b can always be chosen such that the first argument can be written as x_1 in the base period. (Also notice for this section $u(\cdot)$ is a function of n arguments. This notation is inconsistent with that of later sections but no confusion should follow.)

[11] If ψ is a scalar-valued function of the vector w, then $\psi(\cdot)$ is said to be (strictly) quasi-concave if for each scalar ξ the set $\{w : \psi(w) \geqslant \xi\}$ is (strictly) convex. See Arrow and Enthoven (1961).

[12] Equation (3.10) is an instance of the class of envelope theorems frequently encountered in the constrained minimization (and maximization) problems of economics. For a discussion of envelope theorems, see Samuelson (1947, pp. 34–5).

[13] Note that there are two effects. An increase in b makes it cheaper today to attain a given utility level, but it also raises the utility level which would have been achieved with yesterday's income and prices. If we were analyzing quality change rather than taste change, only the former effect would be present.

[14] More complicated theorems can be derived from Theorem 3.1, Corollary 3.1, and Lemma 3.6 (or from Theorem 3.2 using the chain property of the true cost-of-living index). For example, we know that if demand for the first good is price elastic and its price has risen $(p_1 > \hat{p}_1)$ and if we know that prices have risen for all goods that are gross complements for the first and have fallen for all goods that are gross substitutes for the first good, then we know that $(\partial y/\partial b) > 0$. (Assuming, of course, that for the relevant values of prices, all goods other than the first remain either gross complements or gross substitutes for the first good. The assumption that the sign of $\eta_{j1}, j = 2, \ldots, n$, or of $(\eta_{11} + 1)$ does not change when prices change is implicit in much of the discussion that follows.)

[15] It may be thought that these results are obvious. It is natural to expect, for example, that in the situation being analyzed substitutes for the first good will decline in importance and complements will increase. While it is clear that one should indeed expect this as part of the intuitive

meaning of 'substitutes', however, it is not at all clear to us that one would automatically apply such intuition to *gross* substitutes rather than to *net* substitutes or to substitutes defined in yet some different way.

[16] As before, it is implicitly assumed that we remain in ranges of prices in which the elasticity stays on the same side of minus unity and substitute-complement relationships are not reversed.

[17] If the first good is not inferior, certain cases are ruled out. Thus, in this case, the *j*th good must be a net substitute for the first good if it is also a gross substitute. Similarly, if the demand for the first good is inelastic, η_{11}^n must be greater than -1.

[18] The systems (4.1)–(4.4), (4.9), and (4.5)–(4.8) are the well-known conditions of Kuhn-Tucker-Lagrange (KTL). The assumption of nonsatiation of consumption guarantees that if (4.1)–(4.9) is solved for y then $(y/\hat{y})$ is the true cost-of-living index. The proof of the optimality of KTL for quasi-concave programming problems with nonsatiation is given in Arrow and Enthoven (1961, pp. 783–8). Nonsatiation also implies that the equilibrium values of λ and $\hat{\lambda}$ are positive.

[19] Arrow (1958, p. 85) discusses the use of demand reservation prices in the construction of a cost-of-living index.

[20] We have already discussed the problem of deciding whether to treat a given change as one in quality or one in tastes. There is a less basic decision as to whether a change in quality should be treated as such or as the appearance of a new good and the disappearance of an old one. This decision (unlike the former one) is largely a matter of convenience. In this section, we assume that it has been made in favor of retaining the same name (or subscript) for a good before and after the change, i.e. in favor of treating the change as one in the quality of a given good.

[21] The use of hedonic price indices (see the references in note 1) is the most sophisticated way now known of using such market information to obtain price adjustments for quality change. It should come as no surprise that the extension of the results of hedonic price index investigations outside the sample period in which the market observations are made is strictly appropriate only in the repackaging case. The theory of hedonic price indices treats a new quality of a given good as a repackaging of a bundle of underlying attributes. Only if the attributes enter the utility function through the 'package' rather than directly, will hedonic price index adjustments be more than locally appropriate. Obviously, to say this is not to disparage the usefulness of hedonic price indices in practice.

[22] For many purposes it is simpler to regard refrigerator services as entering the utility function directly than it is to leave them out. Consumer theory deals with goods traded in the market place, not with later composites of them made up by consumers (such as home-refrigerated ice cream). In any case, to say that refrigerators enter directly rather than

through other goods is a matter of notation at the level of abstraction of most treatments of consumer theory.

[23] There is no reason other than one of convenience why b has to be a scalar. Quality change may take place in more than one attribute of the first good, in which case b would be replaced by $(b_1, \ldots, b_k)$ and the analysis would be essentially unchanged.

[24] It may be noted that the present problem differs from that of taste changes discussed in section III above in that the change in the utility function is 'embodied' in the first good rather than being 'disembodied'. The parallel to models of embodied and disembodied technical change in production functions is obvious, extending the well-known parallel between the theory of the utility-maximizing consumer and the theory of the cost-minimizing firm. Indeed, some of the results of this section also parallel some of the results in the analysis of such models. We shall return to this in a later footnote.

[25] We assume that $u(\cdot)$ is a strictly quasi-concave function of its first n (nonnegative) arguments and restrict our attention to interior minima.

[26] Note that the result is just that which would be obtained ignoring the effects of b on x. Thus a small unit increase in b raises u by u_b which allows a decrease in expenditure by u_b/λ, since $1/\lambda$ is the marginal cost of a unit of utility. As in the analogous case in section III (and as in the lemma which follows), this is an envelope theorem.

[27] If the new and old varieties of the first good coexist on the same (perfect) market, however, their relative prices will code all the information needed for local adjustment. See the discussion above.

[28] It is natural to take $g(x_1,1) = x_1$, i.e. $g^*(x_1,1) = 1$, but this is not required for our results.

[29] The situation is very similar to that in models of embodied technical change in which a capital aggregate is to be formed or the effect of technical change removed by the use of a quality-corrected capital index, that is, by adjusting the prices of capital goods of different vintages. Under constant returns, technical change must be capital augmenting, analogous to part (B) of the theorem. Under a generalized form of constant returns in which the production functions are homogeneous of degree one in labor and some function of capital, technical change must be capital-altering, a kind of change analogous to the variable repackaging of part (A) of the theorem. See Fisher (1965).

[30] It is natural to take $g(x_1, \ldots, x_m, 1) = x_1$, i.e. $g^*(x_1, \ldots, x_m,1) = 1$, but this is not required for our results.

[31] It is natural to take $g(x_1,x_2,1) = x_2 = g(0,x_2,b)$, i.e. $g^*(x_1,x_2,1) = 1 = g^*(0,x_2,1)$, but this is not required for our results.

[32] It is natural to take $g^1(x_1,1) = x_1$ and $g^i(x_1,x_i,1) = x_i = g^i(0,x_i,b)$

$(i = 2, \ldots, n)$, i.e. $g^{*1}(x_1,1) = 1$ and $g^{*i}(x_1,x_i,1) = 1 = g^{*i}(0,x_i,b)$ $(i = 2, \ldots, n)$, but this is not required for our results.

[33] If $g_1^1 = 0$ in some open neighborhood in the $x_1 - b$ plane in which $g_b^1 \neq 0$, then b enters the utility function in that neighborhood in some way other than by augmenting the services of the commodities.

[34] If g^1 takes the form of (B) of Theorem 5.3, only dependence on the first commodity is involved; if g^1 takes the form of (B) of Theorem 5.1, the percentage adjustment in p_1 is a constant.

[35] This is quite general in the small, but not in the large.

[36] Is it really much more difficult to say, for example, how the introduction of larger, more powerful cars affects the enjoyment of the services of other prestige items than it is to say how such introduction affects the enjoyment of the services of cars? Both evaluations seem hard to make, but the second one is made in practice. Admittedly, however, the second evaluation can be made implicitly through the use of market data if new and 'old' (but not necessarily used) cars sell on the same perfect market. Even then, as we have seen, that adjustment will generally only suffice while that market situation lasts.

REFERENCES FOR ESSAY I

Adelman, I. and Griliches, Z. 1961. "On an index of quality change." *Journal of the American Statistical Association* **56**, 535–548.

Afriat, S. N. 1963. "An identity concerning the relation between the Paasche and Laspeyre indices." *Metroeconomica* **15**, 136–140.

———. 1967. "The cost of living index." In *Essays in Mathematical Economics in Honor of Oskar Morgenstern* (Martin Shubik, ed.), pp. 335–365. Princeton University Press, Princeton, New Jersey.

Allen, R. G. D. 1963. "Price index numbers." *Review of the International Statistical Institute* **31**, 281–297.

———. 1935. "Some observations on the theory and practice of price index numbers." *Review of Economic Studies* **3**, 57–66.

———. 1949. "The economic theory of index numbers." *Economica* N.S., **16**, 197–203.

Arrow, K. J. 1958. "The measurement of price changes." In *The Relationship of Prices to Economic Stability and Growth*, U.S. Congress, Joint Economic Committee, pp. 77–88. Government Printing Office, Washington.

———. and Enthoven, A. C. 1961. Quasi-concave programming. *Econometrica* **19**, 250–272.

Bailey, M. J., Muth, R. F., and Nourse, H. O. 1963. "A regression method for real estate price index construction." *Journal of the American Statistical Association* **58**, 933–942.

Bergstrom, A. R. 1955. "The use of index numbers in demand analysis." *Review of Economic Studies* **23**, 17–26.

Bowley, A. L. 1928. "Notes on index numbers." *Economic Journal* **38**, 216–237.

———. 1938. "Note on Professor Frisch's 'The problem of index numbers'." *Econometrica* **6**, 83–84.

Burgess, R. W. 1928. "Some important principles of index number construction." *Journal of the American Statistical Association* [Supplement], **23**, 79–82.

Burstein, M. L. 1961. "Measurement of quality change in consumer durables." *Manchester School of Economics and Social Studies* **29**, 267–279.

Cagan, P. 1965. "Measuring quality changes and the purchasing power of money: An exploratory study of automobiles." *National Banking Review* **3**, 217–236.

Court, A. T. 1939. "Hedonic price indexes with automotive examples." In *The Dynamics of Automobile Demand*, pp. 99–117. General Motors Corporation, New York.

Cramer, J. S. 1966. "Een prijsindex van nieuwe personenauto's, 1950–1965." *Statistica Neerlandica* **20**, 215–239.

Dacy, D. C. 1964. "A price and productivity index for a nonhomogeneous product." *Journal of the American Statistical Association* **59**, 469–480.

Davies, G. R. 1932. "Index numbers in mathematical economics." *Journal of the American Statistical Association* [Supplement], **27**, 58–64.

Dean, C. R., and DePodwin, H. J. 1961. "Product variation and price indexes: A case study of electrical apparatus." *Proceedings of the Business and Economic Statistics Section* pp. 271–279. American Statistical Association, Washington.

Dhrymes, P. J. 1967. "On the measurement of price and quality changes in some consumer capital goods." *American Economic Review* **57**, 501–518.

Edgeworth, F. Y. 1925. "The plurality of index numbers." *Economic Journal* **35**, 379–388.

Fettig, L. P. 1963. "Adjusting farm tractor prices for quality changes, 1950–1962." *Journal of Farm Economics* **45**, 599–611.

Fisher, F. M. 1965. "Embodied technical change and the existence of an aggregate capital stock." *Review of Economic Studies* **32**, 263–288.

———. and Shell, K. 1967. "Taste and quality change in the pure theory of the true cost-of-living index." In *Value, Capital, and Growth: Essays in Honour of Sir John Hicks* (J. N. Wolfe, ed.) pp. 97–140. University of Edinburgh Press, Edinburgh.

Fisher, I. 1922. *The Making of Index Numbers*. Houghton, Boston, Massachusetts.

Gavett, T. W. 1967. "Quality and a pure price index." *Monthly Labor Review* **90**, 16–20.

Gorman, W. M. 1967. "Tastes, habits and choices." *International Economic Review* **8**, 218–222.

Griliches, Z. 1961. "Hedonic price indexes for automobiles: An econometric analysis of quality change." In *The Price Statistics of the Federal Government*, General Series, No. 73, pp. 137–196. National Bureau of Economic Research, New York.

———. 1964. "Notes on the measurement of price and quality changes." In *Models of Income Determination*, Studies in Income and Wealth, Vol. 28, pp. 301–404. National Bureau of Economic Research, Princeton, New Jersey.

———. 1967. "Hedonic price indexes revisited: Some notes on the state of the art." *Proceedings of the Business and Economic Statistics Section*, pp. 324–332. American Statistical Association, Washington.

Haberler, G. 1927. *Der Sinn der Indexzahlen*. Verlag von J. C. B. Mohr (Paul Siebeck), Tübingen.

———. 1929. "Der volkswirtschaftliche Geldwert und die Preisindexziffern, eine Erwiderung." *Weltwirtschaftliches Archiv* **30**, 6**–14**.

Hicks, J. R. 1942. "Consumers' surplus and index-numbers." *Review of Economic Studies* **9**, 126–137.

Hofsten, E. von. 1952. *Price Indexes and Quality Changes*. Bokforlaget Forum AB, Stockholm.

Hoover, E. D. 1961. "The CPI and problems of quality change." *Monthly Labor Review* **84**: 1175–1185.

Houthakker, H. S. 1951–52. "Compensated changes in quantities and qualities consumed." *Review of Economic Studies* **19**, 155–164.

Joseph, M. F. W. 1936. "Further notes on index numbers, II. Mr. Lerner's supplementary limits for price index numbers." *Review of Economic Studies* **3**, 155–157.

Kemp, M. C. 1957. "Index numbers and demand analysis." *Review of Economic Studies* **24**, 198–202.

Klein, L. R., and Rubin, H. 1947–48. "A constant utility index of the cost of living." *Review of Economic Studies* **15**, 84–87.

Konüs, A. A. 1924. "The problem of the true index of the cost of living." (In Russian.) *The Economic Bulletin of the Institute of Economic Conjuncture*, Moscow, No. 9–10, 64–71. English translation (1939): *Econometrica* **7**, 10–29.

Lancaster, K. 1966. "A new approach to consumer theory." *Journal of Political Economy* **74**, 132–157.

———. 1966. "Change and innovation in the technology of consumption." *American Economic Review* **56**, 14–23.

Larsgaard, O. A., and Mack, L. J. 1961. "Compact cars in the consumer price index." *Monthly Labor Review* **84**, 522–523.

Leontief, W. W. 1936. "Composite commodities and the problem of index numbers." *Econometrica* **4**, 39–59.

———. 1947a. Introduction to a theory of the internal structure of functional relationships. *Econometrica* **15**, 361–373.

———. 1947b. A note on the interrelation of subsets of independent variables of a continuous function with continuous first derivatives. *Bulletin of the American Mathematical Society* **53**, 343–350.

Lerner, A. P. 1935. "A note on the theory of price index numbers." *Review of Economic Studies* **3**, 50-56.

————. 1936. "Further notes on index numbers, III. A reply." *Review of Economic Studies* **3**, 157–158.

Mack L. J. 1955. "Automobile prices in the consumer price index." *Monthly Labor Review* **72**, 5.

Malmquist, S. 1953. "Index numbers and indifference surfaces." *Trabajos de Estadistica* **4**, 209–242.

Muellbauer, J. N. J. "The 'pure theory of true cost of living index' revisited." Warwick Economic Research Papers No. 15, University of Warwick, England.

————. 1971. "The theory of 'true' input price indices." Warwick Economic Research Papers No. 17, University of Warwick, England.

Nicholson, J. L. 1967. "The measurement of quality changes." *Economic Journal* **77**, 512–530.

Price Statistics of the Federal Government, The. 1961. General Series, No. 73. National Bureau of Economic Research, New York. Also published as U.S. Congress, Joint Economic Committee, *Government Price Statistics, Hearings*, 87th Congress, 1st session, Part 1, Jan. 24, 1961. Government Printing Office, Washington. (Cited as *Price Statistics* 1961.)

Richter, M. K. 1966. "Invariance axioms and economic indexes." *Econometrica* **34**, 749–755.

Samuelson, P. A. 1947. *Foundations of Economic Analysis.* Harvard University Press, Cambridge, Massachusetts.

————. 1950. "Evaluation of real national income." *Oxford Economic Papers* N.S., **1**, 1–29.

Schultz, H. 1939. "A misunderstanding in index number theory: The true Konüs condition on cost-of-living index numbers and its limitations." *Econometrica* **7**, 1–9.

Staehle, H. 1935. "A development of the economic theory of price index numbers." *Review of Economic Studies* **3**, 163–188.

————. 1936. "Further notes on index numbers. I." *Review of Economic Studies* **3**, 153–155.

————. 1937. "A general method for the comparison of the price of living." *Review of Economic Studies* **4**, 205–214.

Stone, R. 1956. *Quantity and Price Indexes in National Accounts.* Organization for European Economic Co-operation, Paris.

Strotz, R. H. 1955–56. Myopia and inconsistency in dynamic utility maxization. *Review of Economic Studies* **23**, 165–180.

Triplett, J. E. 1969. "Automobiles and hedonic quality measurement." *Journal of Political Economy* **77**, 408–417.

Ulmer, M. J. 1946. "On the economic theory of cost of living index numbers." *Journal of the American Statistical Association* **41**, 530–542.

U.S. Congress, Joint Economic Committee. 1961. *Government Price Statistics, Hearings*, 87th Congress, 1st session, Part 2, May 1–5, 1961. Government Printing Office, Washington. (For Part 1, See *Price Statistics* 1961.)

von Hofsten, E. A. G. 1952. *Price indexes and quality changes*. Stockholm.

Wald, A. 1937. "Zur Theorie der Preisindexziffern." *Zeitschrift für National-ökonomie* **8**, 179–219.

———. 1939. "A new formula for the index of cost of living." *Econometrica* **7**, 319–331.

The Pure Theory of the National Output Deflator

I. *Introduction*

While the economic theory of the cost-of-living index is firmly grounded in the theory of the consumer,[1] apparently no similar agreed-upon foundation for the other principal type of price index number construction —the deflation of money output by a price index to obtain a measure of real output—exists. Yet the construction of a national output deflator is an enterprise of equal importance to the construction of a cost-of-living index, and it therefore seems desirable to consider that construction in the light of the theory of production in a fashion parallel to the consideration of the cost-of-living index in the light of the theory of consumption. Among other things, such a consideration should illuminate the relationships between the deflators actually constructed with market data and the production-theoretic index or indices that one might wish to construct given more complete information about the technical capabilities of the economy. It should also assist in the analysis of the effects which technical change and the introduction of new goods ought to have on such actually constructed deflators.[2]

This essay provides such a theory, which turns out to be isomorphic in most important respects to the pure theory of the cost-of-living index. That isomorphism allows us to draw on the latter theory, particularly in the consideration of technical change where the interpretation of our earlier work on taste changes in the theory of the cost-of-living index (Fisher and Shell, 1968, which appears as Essay I in this volume) turns out to have a natural and immediate interpretation.

There are two points which it will be wise to get out of the way before beginning our analysis, however. As must already be clear, we believe that it is important to ground price index construction in economic theory; in particular, to ground the construction of output deflators in the theory of production. While we are not the first to take this view (see, for example, Richter 1966), we are going to emphasize it and to argue that existing practices should be considered only as approximations to a theoretically sound index. Yet, unlike the case of the cost-of-living index, where such a view is both natural and long accepted, this view of output deflation may not seem instantly compelling, especially to those directly concerned with index number construction. This is not unreasonable. Any scalar measure of real output and associated measure of price change must contain some arbitrary elements. If one wishes to take the position that what he "really" means by real GNP is current output valued in base-year prices, that position is entirely tenable and it is fruitless to argue that what is "really" meant is something else. While, of course, we believe that the indices here discussed are in some sense more natural and appealing than are real GNP (in the usual sense) and the corresponding GNP deflator, and that the usually computed indices should be considered as approximations to ours in the same way that the consumer price index is considered an approximation to the true cost-of-living index, there is no point in inviting semantic controversy, and the definitions of the GNP deflator and real GNP are well established. For this reason, in the following analysis we shall refer to indices of national output and to a national output deflator.

Secondly, we shall be considering the production-theoretic analysis of national output deflation. A different analysis can be (and has been) given in terms of the arithmetic properties that one might want such a deflator to have (transitivity, for example). While our indices do have some of those properties (when properly considered), our analysis is properly an exercise in production theory rather than in the theory of 'ideal index number' construction.

II. *Real Output Indices and Production Possibility Maps*
Suppose that there are factors of production $v_1, \ldots, v_m$ and outputs $x_1, \ldots, x_r$. Let v and x be the column vectors of the v_i and x_j, respectively. Let the technology at time 0 (the base year) be given by

$$F(x, v) = 0. \tag{2.1}$$

For the present, assume that at time 0, the factor endowments v are inelastically supplied and fixed in amount,[3] say at v^0. Then the production possibility frontier (PPF) at time 0 is given by

$$F(x, v^0) = 0. \tag{2.2}$$

Consider now all the PPF's which could be generated by factor endowments in the proportions given by v^0 but in different absolute amounts. That is, consider for any positive scalar μ the PPF given by

$$F(x, \mu v^0) = 0. \tag{2.3}$$

We shall call the set of such frontiers the *production possibility map* (PPM) at time 0. It shows what efficient combinations of outputs would be with the technology of time 0 and "doses" of the factor endowments of that time applied in different amounts. Naturally, if all production functions exhibit constant returns, F will be homogeneous of degree zero in x and μ, and the PPM will be homothetic. Such homotheticity can also arise in other ways. For the present, we need not assume homotheticity.

It will be convenient and reasonable, but not strictly necessary, to assume that (2.3) can be solved for μ as a function of x and v^0. Since v^0 is constant, we shall suppress it and write the PPF for any value of μ as the set of x such that

$$\phi(x) = \mu. \tag{2.4}$$

The function ϕ can be regarded as a factor requirements function which for any bundle of outputs x gives the minimum dosage of factors (in the proportions stated by v^0) which is required to produce it.

Now suppose that, with $\mu = 1$, output is originally at some bundle x^A (see Figure 2.1). Prices are p^A (a column vector) and money output is

$$y^A \equiv p^{A\prime} x^A. \tag{2.5}$$

Naturally, the line (or hyperplane) (2.5) is tangent to the PPF at x^A.[4]

Suppose that there is no change in either technology or the proportions in which factor endowments occur, so that the PPM and the function $\phi(x)$ are unchanged. Suppose further that output then moves to a different point x^B on the *same* PPF ($\mu = 1$) as x^A. This occurs because prices have shifted from p^A to p^B. It is thus natural (but not inevitable) to regard the resulting shift in money output, from y^A to $y^B \equiv p^{B\prime} x^B$ as entirely a 'monetary' phenomenon and to say that real output has not changed at all. We shall adopt this position.[5]

Reasonable as this position is, however, it carries implications which at first may seem disturbing. If x^A and x^B are judged to have the same real

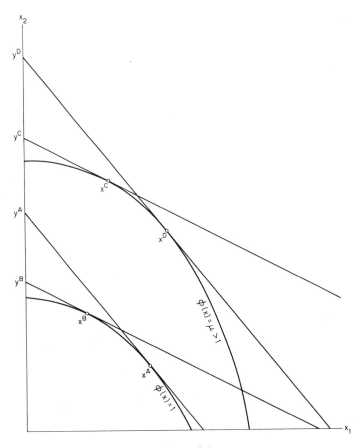

Figure 2.1

national output because they are on the same PPF, it follows immediately that comparison of real national output at those (or any) points cannot depend solely on observed prices and outputs. It also depends on the PPM with which the comparison is made. Thus, for example, there is no reason why with a different technology or a different set of relative factor endowments, the PPF through x^A could not pass above x^B. In this case, even though prices p^B might call forth outputs x^B, we would certainly say that real national output had decreased in the move from x^A to x^B. Similarly, a case can readily be generated in which real national output increases in the same move. There is nothing particularly disturbing about this once we realize that real national output comparisons must necessarily be arbitrary in some degree and that the natural-appearing choice which we have adopted makes such comparisons from the point of view of a particular PPM. In effect, in each comparison we are asking whether the production system that produced x^A would have to be expanded, contracted, or left unchanged to produce x^B.

Such dependence on the PPM can readily be used to generate seeming anomalies.[6] Thus, for example, suppose that the initial situation (in which x^A was produced) is that pictured in Figure 2.1. Then a movement to x^B will be regarded as no change in real national output. Suppose, however, that after the move takes place, the PPM shifts and the new PPF through x^B passes above x^A. Then we shall apparently be saying that real national output at x^A has two different values. Obviously, this comes from trying to chain together two different things: a comparison made with the PPM which obtained when x^A was produced and one made with the PPM which obtained when x^B was. Had the first map remained unchanged, the comparison would clearly have been transitive.

Moreover, as we shall see in more detail a bit later on, if *with the second map* production had shifted back to x^A, then there is a real sense in which the entire move from x^A to x^B and back to x^A *has* decreased real national output. The prices at which x^A will be produced with the new PPM will no longer be p^A, but a different set of prices; and had those prices obtained originally, the value of production would have been greater than it now is at x^A. But of this, more in a moment.

We return now to the case of an unchanging PPM and inquire about comparisons of points not on the same PPF. Thus, suppose that with no change in technology or factor endowment proportions, output is observed to move from x^A to x^C, *not* on the same PPF as x^A (see Figure 2.1). Suppose, as before, that prices move from p^A to p^B. Money output becomes $y^C \equiv p^{B'} x^C$. Clearly, in this situation, it is natural to regard the change in relative money output as composed of

$$\left(\frac{y^C}{y^A}\right) = \left(\frac{y^B}{y^A}\right)\left(\frac{y^C}{y^B}\right), \tag{2.6}$$

and to regard the first factor on the right as the appropriate money output deflator and the second as a measure of increase in real output.

Now, we have not drawn x^C on the same ray through the origin as x^B in Figure 2.1, because we have not assumed the PPM to be homothetic. This immediately raises the possibility that our decomposition (2.6) of the move from x^A to x^C may not be unique. Thus, consider the PPF through $x^C(\phi(x) = \mu > 1)$. This is tangent at x^C to the price line corresponding to prices p^B. We can clearly start with this PPF as a base and look for that point on it which would have been produced with the original prices p^A. Call that point x^D and the associated value $y^D \equiv p^{A'} x^D$. Then the change in relative money output from y^A to y^C can be decomposed as

$$\left(\frac{y^C}{y^A}\right) = \left(\frac{y^D}{y^A}\right)\left(\frac{y^C}{y^D}\right), \tag{2.7}$$

and the first factor on the right measures the increase in real output while the second is a money output deflator.

If the PPM is homothetic, then the two decompositions (2.6) and (2.7) generate the same real output index and the same deflator. If the map is not homothetic, then two different indices are generated, even from a single PPM. The situation is precisely the same as in the theory of the cost-of-living index, where a nonhomothetic indifference map generates two equally sound indices, one starting from today's and one from yesterday's indifference curve (see Essay I, especially pp. 2–7). The case in the present analysis differs only in that there may be more reason to be interested in homotheticity of the PPM than of the indifference map.

An illuminating way to look at the matter in the nonhomothetic case is to see that the two sets of indices answer different questions. The decomposition in (2.6) corresponds to asking what the economy which possessed just the right resources to produce x^A when prices were p^A would have produced if prices had been p^B. The decomposition (2.7), on the other hand, corresponds to asking what the economy which in fact produced x^C when prices were p^B would have produced had prices been p^A. In the homothetic case, the indices derived from the answers to these questions happen to coincide, but they are, of course, different questions nonetheless.

Considering the matter in this way, it becomes clear how to deal with the problem when the PPM changes. (This is of crucial importance not only because technology changes over time but also because the very process of investment alters the vector v^0 and thus the PPM.) Nothing in the discussion above really depended on an unchanged PPM. There is no reason why the PPF through x^C had to come from the same PPM as that through x^A. If it does not, then the two decompositions (2.6) and (2.7) correspond to two sets of output indices and deflators coming from two different PPM's.

It is clear, of course, that neither real output index depends solely on the PPM. That would be impossible, in general, given the scalar nature of an index. Rather, each index even of *real* output depends also on prices. In particular, the real output index starting with x^A depends on p^B and the real output index starting with x^C depends on p^A. The reason for this has already been indicated, but a slightly different discussion may make it appear more reasonable.

What we count as part of real output does not depend solely on production possibilities. The fact that many widgets could be produced does not affect real output unless widgets happen to be something that people are interested in buying. Similarly, items which consumers value highly should and do count more heavily in a real output index than items which they value relatively little. Prices, of course, give the rates at which purchasers are just willing to trade one good for another and it is clear that with a given set of prices, a particular isovalue line gives the locus of points of equal real output by giving the locus of points which purchasers value equally. It is true that the trade-offs given by the price ratios in fact hold only locally, but just as in constructing a cost-of-living index we ignore production (except as revealed through prices) and take a given price line as representing the opportunity locus, so in constructing a real output index we ignore tastes (except as revealed through prices) and take a given price line as representing a locus of constant value.

Looked at in this way, the index beginning with the PPF through x^A is relevant in answering the question: What is the capacity of the economy which produced value y^A when prices were p^A to produce the things now valued at prices p^B? A similar question corresponds to the other index.[7]

That these two indices are designed to answer different questions and that they depend on prices and the PPM can be well pointed up by explicit consideration of an apparently anomalous case. In Figure 2.2, the initial PPF is drawn. With prices p^A, production is at x^A and money output at y^A. Now suppose that prices change to p^B and that we observe the *same* production point as before, x^A, but a new money output, y^C. Using the initial PPF, we conclude that the change in money output is not merely a price phenomenon. With that frontier, had prices been p^B, production would have been at x^B and money output at y^B. The fact that money output is only at y^C means that real output has decreased. This may seem strange, but it is entirely reasonable. The capacity of the economy to produce value

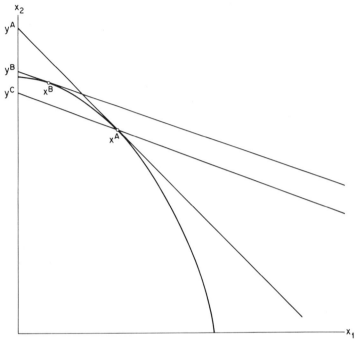

Figure 2.2

at prices p^B has decreased. In terms of the valuation now placed by purchasers on goods, real output has indeed gone down; the new PPF lies inside the old PPF in the relevant range.

On the other hand, if we begin with prices p^B and money output y^C and use the *new* PPF (not drawn), we will find that real output has increased. But this is real output valued at prices p^A, which is not the same thing at all. The capacity of the economy to produce value, given the *old* valuations, has indeed gone up and the new PPF lies outside the old PPF in the range relevant to that valuation. There is nothing contradictory in this.

III. *Which Index Is Relevant?*

The example just given suggests that while our two indices have equal intellectual footing, they may not be of equal relevance for all purposes. Clearly, such equality must appear when geographical comparisons are in view; it need not appear when we are interested in changes over time.

The reason for this is that one index compares real outputs using today's valuations whereas the other makes the comparisons using yesterday's valuations. Yet if we consider planning ahead, these are not equally relevant. Thus, suppose that we consider alternative policies which will result in different outputs tomorrow. If we are interested in which policy will give the higher real output, it is clear that we want to make the comparison using the valuations which will *then* obtain.[8] The fact that Policy I leads to an economy whose ability to produce items now valued is less than that of the economy which will result from Policy II is of no moment if those valuations will no longer apply. Crudely put, the two policies ought to be compared as to ability to produce what people want, not as to ability to produce what they used to want. It is possible but not particularly appealing to say that real output has gone down because suits of armor are no longer produced. Thus the index based on yesterday's capacity to produce items valued today seems the more relevant one.[9]

Naturally, however, the other index is not without interest, and we shall want to see in what way the two indices differ. This will be of practical importance, for it bears on the properties of Paasche and Laspeyres indices.

IV. *Paasche and Laspeyres Indices*
It is obviously of interest to see how our indices are related to the usual Paasche and Laspeyres indices. This is quite easy to do. In Figure 4.1, with

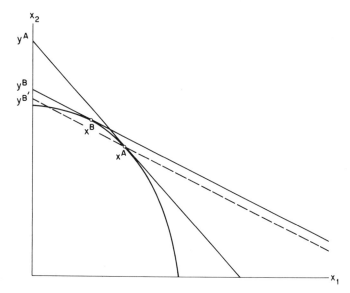

Figure 4.1

prices p^A and the PPF as drawn, production was initially at x^A and money output at y^A. Prices now shift to p^B. With the same PPF, production would be at x^B and money output at y^B, so our deflator based on yesterday's PPM and today's valuations will be given by (y^B/y^A).

Now consider the Laspeyres price index given by $(y^{B'}/y^A)$ where $y^{B'} \equiv p^{B'} x^A$. Since x^B maximizes value at prices p^B subject to the constraint of being on the PPF, and since x^A is on that PPF, it is clear that $y^{B'} \leqslant y^B$, with the strict inequality holding if the production set is strictly convex.

Thus, *a Laspeyres* price *index* understates *the deflator based on yesterday's* PPM *and today's valuations.* Since the product of a Laspeyres *price* and a Paasche *quantity* index gives the change in money output, it follows that *a Paasche* quantity *index* overstates *the change in real output measured on the same basis.*

Similarly, by an essentially identical argument, a Paasche price index *overstates* the deflator based on today's PPM and yesterday's valuations; a Laspeyres quantity index *understates* the correspondingly computed change in real output.

It is interesting to note that these relationships are just the reverse of those which occur in the case of a cost-of-living index.[10] In that case, as is well known, a Paasche price index understates and a Laspeyres price index overstates the relevant cost-of-living index. In that case, also, not one but two indices are involved, with the Paasche index bounding below the cost-of-living index based on today's budget constraint and today's tastes and the Laspeyres index bounding above the cost-of-living index based on yesterday's budget constraint and yesterday's tastes. (If the indifference map does not change, 'indifference curve' should be substituted for 'tastes' in the preceding sentence.) We argued in Essay I that if tastes change, the interesting cost-of-living index is the one bounded by the Paasche price index rather than the one bounded by the Laspeyres index. In the present case, the reverse is true if the PPM changes. It is the index bounded by the Laspeyres price index which is the relevant deflator.[11]

We may remark that the actual practice is to compute the consumer price index as a Laspeyres index and the implicit GNP deflator as a Paasche index. If it is accepted that the former index is an approximation to the cost-of-living index based on consumer theory and the latter an approximation to the real output deflator based on production theory as discussed here, then in both cases the published indices have an inflationary bias, despite (indeed because of) their different methods of computation. If, in addition, we accept the arguments in Essay I as to which of the two theoretically based cost-of-living indices is the relevant one when tastes change and the argument of the present paper as to which of the two real output deflators is the appropriate one when the PPM changes, then in both cases the published index imparts an inflationary bias to a theoretically based index which is not the relevant one. Their relation to the relevant indices when tastes or production possibilities change is in general unknown.[12] It would seem to be better to compute the Consumer Price Index as a Paasche index and the GNP deflator as a Laspeyres index.

Returning to real output deflation, as we have just seen, a Laspeyres price index bounds the more relevant theoretical index from below while a Paasche price index bounds the less relevant one from above. Clearly, it would be desirable to have an upper bound on the more relevant index as well. To accomplish this (in effect, to see how a Paasche index might be altered to make it bound that index) is possible if one knows something about the way in which the PPM changes. A principal aim of the present paper is to analyze some leading cases of such changes; this is done in later sections.

v. *Market Imperfections and Underutilized Resources*

Before proceeding, it may be useful to clear up one point by indicating that our analysis is in fact not wholly dependent on a restrictive-appearing assumption. This is the assumption of perfect competition—more generally, the assumption that the economy operates on the PPF.

This is not hard to handle, at least in part. Recall that our PPM is generated by taking different values of the 'dose' level μ in the equation

$$\phi(x) = \mu \tag{5.1}$$

where the function $\phi(x)$ is defined relative to a vector of fixed available resources v^0. The PPF is obtained by setting $\mu = 1$. If the economy operates on the PPF, then, as seen above, we can form our indices by using that frontier—formally, by using the production possibility curve which is just tangent to the value line $y = p'x$ where p and y are actual prices and money output, respectively.

If, on the other hand, the economy operates inside the frontier, then one possibility is to continue to form our indices in essentially the same manner.

In this case, however, the production possibility curve tangent to the actual value line will *not* be the production possibility *frontier* ($\mu = 1$), but the curve for some lower value of μ. (That value can, incidentally, be taken as an index of the underutilization or misallocation of resources.) It is the case, of course, that particularly when markets are imperfect, that curve and the actual value line will not generally be tangent at the point of actual production, but this is not important for most of our analysis.

There are, however, alternative ways to proceed. The alternative just discussed essentially proceeded by making the inefficient economy equivalent to an efficient one with the same PPM but a 'dose' level μ just enough to enable it to produce the same value. We might also consider a comparison with an efficient economy with the same map and a level of μ just sufficient to enable it to reach the same production point. That is, we might use the production possibility curve which passes through the point x^A of actual production. This situation is pictured in Figure 5.1. Actual production is x^A and money output is y^A. An efficient economy with the pictured PPF passing through x^A and facing the same prices would produce money

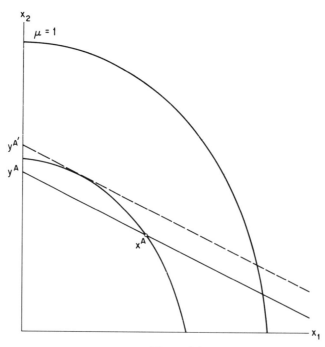

Figure 5.1

output $y^{A'}$. Provided we recognize that such an efficient economy would in fact have a higher real output by the factor $(y^{A'}/y^{A})$, we can use that frontier as the base for much of our analysis. On the other hand, the fact that the chosen production possibility curve and the actual value line are not tangent anywhere creates difficulties for our analysis of the effects of changes in the PPM, given later.[13] In view of this, and in view of the somewhat artificial (but still possible) necessity of remembering that two points (generating money outputs y^{A} and $y^{A'}$) do not have the same real output even though they are on the same production possibility curve because some of that curve is unobtainable, it seems to us that the alternative given earlier (of taking as a base the production possibility curve tangent to the actual value line) is preferable to the present one.

For the case in which inefficiency reflects general underemployment rather than market imperfections, a third alternative is available which is clearly superior to either of the others in most respects. This is to construct the PPM itself with v^0 defined not as the vector of resources *available*, but as the vector of resources *actually utilized*. This obviously results in a PPF tangent to the actual value line at the point of actual production, and our entire analysis goes through without change. Unfortunately, this alternative is not available in the case of inefficiency caused by market imperfections.

For the remainder of this paper, we assume that production is efficient. We have just seen that this assumption is generally only one of convenience.[14]

VI. *The Indices: Formal Description*
We now give a formal description of our real output index and deflator. This need only be done for the deflator, the real output index being obtained by division into the relative change in money output.

We are given initial prices $\hat{p}$, money value of output $\hat{y}$, and a second set of prices p. Given also a particular PPM given by $\{(x, \mu): \phi(x) = \mu > 0\}$, we begin by finding that set of outputs $\hat{x}$ which solves the following problem.

$$\text{Minimize } \mu \text{ subject to } \hat{p}'\hat{x} = \hat{y}. \tag{6.1}$$

Call the resulting value of $\mu, \hat{\mu}$. Now find that vector of outputs x which solves the problem:

$$\text{Maximize } p'x \text{ subject to } \phi(x) = \hat{\mu}. \tag{6.2}$$

Let y be the resulting value of $p'x$; then the deflator is $(y/\hat{y})$.

This apparently cumbersome description is needed for the following reason. When the PPM used is that which actually obtained when $\hat{y}$ was produced at prices $\hat{p}$, the procedure described clearly amounts to finding the actual PPF (and actual outputs $\hat{x}$) and forming the deflator as previously described. When, on the other hand, the PPM used is that which obtained when prices were p, then, *provided that the PPM is homothetic*, the described procedure generates the deflator based on that map and on the actual PPF holding at that time. In the latter case, $\hat{x}$ is not a vector of actually produced outputs but the vector of outputs which would have been produced at prices $\hat{p}$ had the production possibility curve on the new map been just sufficient to generate money output $\hat{y}$ at those prices.

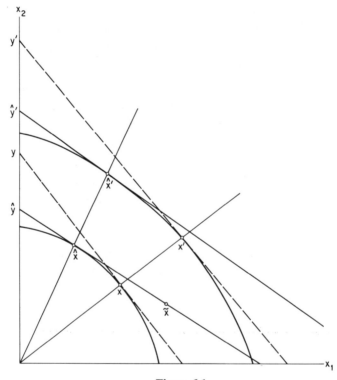

Figure 6.1

The latter situation is pictured in Figure 6.1. The actual PPF is the outer one. Actual production at prices p is at x' and money output at y'. Had prices been $\hat{p}$, actual production would have been at $\hat{x}'$ and money output at $\hat{y}'$. Clearly, the deflator based on this map is $(y'/\hat{y}')$ and this is the same as $(y/\hat{y})$ if the map is homothetic. Actual production in the initial period, however, need not have been at $\hat{x}$, since the PPM was different. In general, it was at some other point on the same value line, say $\tilde{x}$.

If we assume homotheticity, then the described formal procedure enables us to make comparisons of deflators based on different maps by using the calculus. If we do not assume homotheticity, then what is compared is the appropriate deflator from one map with the deflator from the other map, discussed briefly in Section 2, which uses as a base the production possibility curve just sufficient to produce the observed value rather than the actual PPF. The comparison made in the homothetic case is clearly more interesting and we shall henceforth generally assume homotheticity.[15, 16]

VII. *Hicks-Neutral Technological Change*

Assume that the output of the ith good $(i = 1, 2, ..., r)$ depends on the amounts of the m factors devoted to the production of that good. If there are no external economies (or diseconomies) in production, then base-period production possibilities can be described by the system

$$x_i = g^i(v_{i1}, ..., v_{im})$$

$$\sum_{i=1}^{r} v_{ij} \leqslant v_j, \quad v_{ij} \geqslant 0 \quad \text{for } i = 1, 2, ..., r; \, j = 1, 2, ..., m. \quad (7.1)$$

v_{ij} is the amount of the jth factor allocated to the production of the ith good and $g^i(\cdot)$ is the base-period production function for the ith good.

In this section, we focus on an economy which experiences Hicks-neutral technological change (at possibly varying rates) in each of the sectors. For ease of exposition, we begin with the case in which factors are inelastically supplied in equal amounts during the base and current periods, and in which only the production of the first good experiences (Hicks-neutral) technological change. In this special case, the system (7.1) can be rewritten as

$$x_1 = ag^1(v_{11}, ..., v_{1m}),$$

$$x_i = g^i(v_{i1}, ..., v_{im}) \quad \text{for } i = 2, ..., r,$$

$$\sum_{i=1}^{r} v_{ij} \leqslant v_j, \quad v_{ij} \geqslant 0 \quad \text{for } i = 1, 2, ..., r \text{ and } j = 1, 2, ..., m. \quad (7.1')$$

a is then the Hicks-neutral technological efficiency parameter applied to the production of the first good, and units have been chosen so that $a = 1$

in the base period. If, for example, $a > 1$ in the current period, then we say that the production of the first good has experienced Hicks-neutral techno-logical *progress*. Using the notation developed above, it is easy to see that the PPM based on current technology is given by

$$\text{PPM} \equiv \{(x_1, x_2, ..., x_r; \mu) : \phi(x_1/a, x_2, ..., x_r) = \mu > 0\}$$

with the production possibility map depending on the parameter a.

We now turn to the analysis of this economy in terms of the formalism developed in Section 6. The r-dimensional column vector of base-period prices $\hat{p}$, base-period 'money' income $\hat{y}$, the r-dimensional column vector of current prices p, and the PPM defined by current technology are all given data. The first step is to solve for the r-dimensional column vector of outputs, $\hat{x}$, that minimizes factor dosage $\phi(x_1/a, x_2, ..., x_r)$ subject to the requirement that 'money' output in base-period prices, $\hat{p}' \hat{x}$, be equal to the value pro-duced in the base-period, $\hat{y}$. $\hat{x}$ is found by solving the first-order system

$$
\begin{bmatrix}
\hat{p}' \hat{x} \\
\hat{\phi}_1/a \\
\hat{\phi}_2 \\
\cdot \\
\cdot \\
\cdot \\
\hat{\phi}_r
\end{bmatrix}
-
\begin{bmatrix}
\hat{y} \\
\hline
\hat{\lambda}\hat{p}
\end{bmatrix}
= 0, \tag{7.2}
$$

where $\hat{\phi}_i$ $(i = 1, 2, ..., r)$ denotes the derivative of $\phi(\cdot)$ with respect to its ith argument evaluated at $\hat{x}$. Under current technological conditions but with prices at $\hat{p}$ and income at $\hat{y}$, $\hat{\phi}_i$ $(i = 2, ..., r)$ is the required increase in factor dosage μ necessitated by a first-order increase in the production of the ith good; $\hat{\phi}_1/a$ is the required increase in factor dosage necessitated by a first-order increase in the output of the first good. $\hat{\lambda}$ is a nonnegative scalar Lagrange multiplier. $(1/\hat{\lambda})$ can be interpreted as the current marginal cost of factor dosage (in 'money' units) when prices are $\hat{p}$ and value of production is $\hat{y}$.[17]

Defining

$$\hat{\mu} = \phi\left(\frac{\hat{x}_1}{a}, \hat{x}_2, ..., \hat{x}_r\right), \tag{7.3}$$

the next step is to find the r-dimensional column vector of outputs $x = (x_1, x_2, ..., x_r)'$ which maximizes the 'money' value of output subject to the dosage requirement $\phi(x_1/a, x_2, \ldots x_r) = \hat{\mu}$. Thus, x satisfies the first-order conditions

$$
\begin{bmatrix}
\phi \\
\phi_1/a \\
\phi_2 \\
. \\
. \\
. \\
\phi_r
\end{bmatrix}
-
\begin{bmatrix}
\hat{\mu} \\
\text{---} \\
\lambda p
\end{bmatrix}
= 0,
\tag{7.4}
$$

where ϕ_i $(i = 1, 2, \ldots, r)$ denotes the derivative of $\phi(\cdot)$ with respect to its ith argument evaluated at x, and λ is a nonnegative scalar Lagrange multiplier. As before, $(\phi_1/a, \phi_2, \ldots, \phi_r)'$ can be interpreted as the vector of marginal dosage requirements, while $(1/\lambda)$ is interpreted as the marginal 'money' cost of a dose when prices are p and factor availability (measured in doses) is $\hat{\mu}$.

We now observe that the formal analysis of the pure theory of the true national output deflator under Hicks-neutral technological change is isomorphic to that of the pure theory of the true cost-of-living index under good-augmenting taste change (see Essay I, especially Section 3). Maximal utility $\hat{u}$ in the former theory (evaluated at base-period prices and income, but current tastes) is replaced in the present context by the minimal factor dosage $\hat{\mu}$. Current utility at current prices $u(\cdot)$ is replaced by dosage requirement $\phi(\cdot)$. The taste change parameter b is replaced with the inverse of the technological parameter $(1/a)$. We have chosen notation that should allow the reader easily to establish the remainder of the isomorphism.

It should be noted that a similar isomorphism can be established regardless of the choice of preference map on the one hand or the choice of PPM on the other hand. Nor is the isomorphism special to the good-augmenting taste change and Hicks-neutral technological change cases. The isomorphism between the pure theory of the true cost-of-living index and the pure theory of the true national output deflator is completely general, as is the isomorphism between the theory of the utility-maximizing consumer and the theory of the cost-minimizing firm.

Defining $y \equiv p'x$, the true national output deflator is $(y/\hat{y})$. We are interested in how the true national output deflator is affected by technological change. Therefore, we must calculate the full derivative of y with respect to the technological parameter a. Base-period 'money' output $\hat{y}$, base-period prices $\hat{p}$, and current prices p are the given data.

Theorem 7.1.
$$\frac{\partial y}{\partial a} = \frac{p_1 x_1}{a}\left(1 - \frac{\hat{x}_1 \hat{\phi}_1}{x_1 \phi_1}\right).$$

Proof. This is an immediate consequence of the isomorphism just discussed and Theorem 3.1 of Essay I, *mutatis mutandis*. It can also easily be proved as follows.

y is the solution to a constrained maximum problem in which the Lagrangian is

$$L_2 = p'x - \frac{1}{\lambda}\left[\phi\left(\frac{x_1}{a}, x_2, ..., x_r\right) - \hat{\mu}\right]. \tag{7.5}$$

Hence, by the Envelope Theorem (see Samuelson, 1947, pp. 34–35),

$$\frac{\partial y}{\partial a} = \frac{\partial L_2}{\partial a} = \frac{1}{y}\left(\frac{\phi_1 x_1}{a^2} + \frac{\partial \hat{\mu}}{\partial a}\right). \tag{7.6}$$

However, $\hat{\mu}$ is the solution to a constrained minimum problem with Lagrangian

$$L_1 = \phi\left(\frac{\hat{x}_1}{a}, \hat{x}_2, ..., \hat{x}_r\right) - \hat{\lambda}(\hat{p}'\hat{x} - \hat{y}). \tag{7.7}$$

Hence, by the same Envelope Theorem

$$\frac{\partial \hat{\mu}}{\partial a} = \frac{\partial L_1}{\partial a} = \frac{-\hat{\phi}_1 \hat{x}_1}{a^2}. \tag{7.8}$$

Substituting, we obtain

$$\frac{\partial y}{\partial a} = \frac{1}{\lambda}\left(\frac{\phi_1 x_1}{a^2} - \frac{\hat{\phi}_1 \hat{x}_1}{a^2}\right). \tag{7.9}$$

Use of the first-order conditions (7.2) and (7.4) immediately yields the theorem.

The alternative form of the result just obtained in the proof [equation (7.9)] has a straightforward interpretation. We note that $(\hat{x}_1 \hat{\phi}_1/a^2)$ is the *ceteris paribus* decrease in factor dosage when prices are $\hat{p}$ and income is $\hat{y}$ due to a first-order increase in the efficiency parameter a. $(x_1 \phi_1/a^2)$ is the *ceteris paribus* decrease in factor dosage when prices are p and factor dosage is $\hat{\mu}$. Therefore, the terms in the parenthesis on the RHS of (7.9) measure the total change in current factor dosage required to meet the constraint that $\phi(x_1/a, x_2, ..., x_r) = \phi(\hat{x}_1/a, \hat{x}_2, ..., \hat{x}_r)$. Since $(1/\lambda)$ is the current marginal cost (in units, say, of dollars per dose), the entire right-hand side of (7.9) gives the additional dollar value which would be produced today if the economy producing $\hat{y}$ yesterday had in both periods a small change in a.

Corollary 7.1. If $p = \hat{p}$, then $(\partial y/\partial a) = 0$ for all a.

Proof. The corollary is an immediate consequence of Theorem 7.1. By (7.2) and (7.4), if $p = \hat{p}$, then $y = \hat{y}$, so that $x_1 = \hat{x}_1$ and $\phi_1 = \hat{\phi}_1$.

Corollary 7.1 is also an obvious consequence of our definition of the true national output deflator. If prices are unchanged, then in order for the budget lines to be tangent to the same PPF, income must also be unchanged—no matter which PPM is employed as a frame of reference.

We know that $(\partial y/\partial a)$ is zero when current output prices are the same as base-period output prices. Therefore, in studying the effect of technological change upon the national output deflator, it will be helpful to study the qualitative and quantitative behavior of $(\partial y/\partial a)$ as current prices p are displaced from their base-period values $\hat{p}$. First we derive results concerning the sign of $(\partial y/\partial a)$ for values of p different from $\hat{p}$. To do this, it is convenient to define $z(p) \equiv x_1 \phi_1$ and to study the effects of price changes upon $z(p)$.

Several of the results that follow depend upon elasticities of output supply. It will be helpful to agree on some definitions. First define θ_{i1},

$$\theta_{i1} \equiv \frac{p_1}{x_i}\left(\frac{\partial x_i}{\partial p_1}\right)_{y\,\text{const.}}, \quad i = 1, 2, ..., r. \tag{7.10}$$

This is the supply elasticity of the ith good with respect to the price of the first good when 'money' value (equal to 'money' income) is held constant while total factor dosage is allowed to vary. Next, define η_{i1},

$$\eta_{i1} \equiv \frac{p_1}{x_i}\left(\frac{\partial x_i}{\partial p_1}\right)_{\phi = \hat{\mu}\,\text{const.}}, \quad i = 1, 2, ..., r. \tag{7.11}$$

This is the supply elasticity of the ith good with respect to the price of the first good when factor dosage (and thus overall factor supply) is held constant while 'money' value (equal to 'money' income) is allowed to vary.

By analogy with consumer theory, θ_{i1} can be thought of as a *gross* supply elasticity, since value y is held constant, while η_{i1} can be thought of as a *net* supply elasticity, since the calculation is restricted to a given production curve and 'dosage' effects are suppressed. Both θ_{i1} and η_{i1} are in principle obtainable from econometric supply studies. Which of the two supply elasticities is easier to work with in practice? No clear-cut answer can be given to this question. If an econometric study is based on data for which factor supplies change relatively little from observation to observation, then the *net* supply elasticity η_{i1} is probably more natural to estimate. On the other hand, if the data are such that from observation to observation, the 'money' value of output is relatively unchanged, then the *gross* supply elasticity θ_{i1} may be more natural to estimate. Since one can be obtained from the other by a known transformation, neither can be said to be truly preferable; nevertheless, η_{i1} seems to us to measure something more interesting than does θ_{i1}. It measures the supply response of the economy with a fixed production capacity to changes in price.

A third elasticity is often estimated in applied studies, the output supply elasticity where factor supplies are perfectly elastic at fixed prices. However, such partial equilibrium estimates ignore changes in factor prices which must be taken into account in a general equilibrium framework such as the present one. The following theoretical results are thus in terms of θ_{i1} and η_{i1}. Note that, by the Slutsky equation,

$$\theta_{i1} = \eta_{i1} - \frac{p_1 x_1}{x_i}\left(\frac{\partial x_i}{\partial y}\right)_{p\,\text{const.}} . \tag{7.12}$$

Lemma 7.1. If $z(p) = x_1 \phi_1$, then

$$\frac{\partial z}{\partial p_1} = \frac{x_1 \phi_1}{p_1}\{\theta_{11}+1\} \quad \text{and} \quad \frac{\partial z}{\partial p_i} = \frac{x_i \phi_1}{p_1}\theta_{i1}, \quad i = 2,...,r.$$

Proof. This follows directly from Lemma 3.6 of Essay I, *mutatis mutandis*.

Lemma 7.2. If $z = x_1 \phi_1$, then

$$\frac{\partial z}{\partial p_1} = \frac{x_1 \phi_1}{p_1}\left\{\eta_{11} - p_1\left(\frac{\partial x_1}{\partial y}\right)_{p\,\text{const.}} + 1\right\},$$

$$\frac{\partial z}{\partial p_i} = \frac{x_i \phi_1}{p_1}\left\{\eta_{i1} - \frac{p_1 x_1}{x_i}\left(\frac{\partial x_i}{\partial y}\right)_{p\,\text{const.}}\right\} \quad \text{for } i = 2,...,r.$$

Proof. The lemma follows after substituting (7.12) into the results of Lemma 7.1.

Next, define η_{1i}, the net supply elasticity of the first good in terms of the price of the ith good, by

$$\eta_{1i} \equiv \frac{p_i}{x_1}\left(\frac{\partial x_1}{\partial p_i}\right)_{\phi = \hat{\mu}\,\text{const.}}, \quad i = 1, 2, ..., r.$$

Notice, of course, that while substitution effects are symmetric, it is not necessary that the elasticities η_{i1} and η_{1i} be equal, although they certainly must possess the same sign.

Lemma 7.3. If $z = x_1 \phi_1$, then

$$\frac{\partial z}{\partial p_i} = \frac{x_1 \phi_1}{p_i}\left\{\eta_{1i} - p_i\left(\frac{\partial x_i}{\partial y}\right)_{p\,\text{const.}}\right\} \quad \text{for } i = 2, ..., r.$$

Proof. The lemma follows from Lemma 7.2 using the definition of η_{1i} and the symmetry of substitution effects.

We must now agree on some terminology. Define the ith good's share of national income α_i by

$$\alpha_i \equiv \frac{p_i x_i}{y} \quad \text{for } i = 1, 2, ..., r. \tag{7.13}$$

Note that the PPM is homothetic if and only if $(\partial x_i/\partial y)_{p\,\text{const.}} = (x_i/y)$ for $i = 1, 2, ..., r$, and for all positive p and y.

Lemma 7.4. If the PPM is homothetic, then

$$\frac{\partial z}{\partial p_1} = \frac{x_1 \phi_1}{p_1}\{\eta_{11} + 1 - \alpha_1\} \quad \text{and}$$

$$\frac{\partial z}{\partial p_i} = \frac{x_i \phi_1}{p_1}\{\eta_{i1} - \alpha_1\} = \frac{x_1 \phi_1}{p_i}\{\eta_{1i} - \alpha_i\} \quad \text{for } i = 2, ..., r.$$

Proof. $(\partial x_i/\partial y)_{p\,\text{const.}} = (x_i/y)$ as a consequence of the homotheticity of the PPM. Substituting in Lemma 7.2 and Lemma 7.3 and using definition (7.13) completes the proof.

Since substitution effects are symmetric, we know that η_{i1} and η_{1i} share the same sign. From Lemma 7.4, we can further deduce that sign $(\eta_{i1} - \alpha_1) =$ sign $(\eta_{1i} - \alpha_i)$.[18]

In the remainder of this section, we study the implications for the national output deflator of Hicks-neutral technological change under various production conditions. First we study the qualitative effect of Hicks-neutral technological change on the national output deflator for the case in which there is information about the gross supply elasticities $\theta_{i1}, i = 1, 2, ..., r$. It is now not assumed that the PPM is homothetic. The reinstatement of that assumption below enables us greatly to strengthen the results.

Theorem 7.2. (A) Suppose $p_i = \hat{p}_i$ for $i = 2, ..., r$. If $\theta_{11} > -1$, then $(\partial y / \partial a)$ has the same sign as $(p_1 - \hat{p}_1)$. If $\theta_{11} < -1$, then $(\partial y / \partial a)$ has the same sign as $(\hat{p}_1 - p_1)$. If $\theta_{11} = -1$, then $(\partial y / \partial a) = 0$.

(B) Suppose $p_i = \hat{p}_i$ for $i = 1, ..., r$, $i \neq j$, $j \neq 1$. If the jth good is a gross complement to the production of the first good $(\theta_{j1} > 0)$, then $(\partial y / \partial a)$ has the same sign as $(p_j - \hat{p}_j)$. If the jth good is a gross substitute to the production of the first good $(\theta_{j1} < 0)$, then $(\partial y / \partial a)$ has the same sign as $(\hat{p}_j - p_j)$. If $\theta_{j1} = 0$, then $(\partial y / \partial a) = 0$.

(C) If $p_i = k\hat{p}_i$, $i = 1, 2, ..., r$, where k is a positive scalar constant, then $(\partial y / \partial a) = 0$.

Proof. (A) and (B) follow from Theorem 7.1, Corollary 7.1, and Lemma 7.1. (C) Full differentiation of z with respect to k yields

$$k \frac{\partial z}{\partial k} = \phi_1 x_1 + \phi_1 \sum_{i=1}^{r} p_i \left(\frac{\partial x_i}{\partial p_1} \right)_{y \, const.} \tag{7.14}$$

by Lemma 7.1, since $k(\partial p_i / \partial k) = p_i$ by hypothesis. Since $y = p' x$,

$\sum_{i=1}^{r} p_i \left(\frac{\partial x_i}{\partial p_1} \right)_{y \, const.} = -x_1.$ Theorem 7.2(C) follows from Theorem 7.1 and Corollary 7.1.

Notice that Theorem 7.2(A) is a *global* result (that is, a result that holds for all values of p_1) when the sign of $(\theta_{11} + 1)$ is independent of the value of p_1. Theorem 7.2(B) is a global result when the sign of θ_{j1} is independent of the value of p_j. Theorem 7.2(C) is an extension of Corollary 7.1. No matter what the level of the technological parameter a, if current prices are all k times base-period prices, current value y must be equal to k times base-period value $\hat{y}$ in order that tangency with the same PPF be achieved.

The practical importance of Theorem 7.2(A) and (B) is limited by our information on the constant-value supply elasticities θ_{i1} $i = 1, 2, ..., r$. This is probably a severe limitation, since it is difficult to imagine a situation in which it would be natural to estimate directly the supply elasticities θ_{i1}. However, if the θ_{i1} are known, important practical implications follow. Suppose, for example, that all prices save the jth are the same in the two periods. If technology does not change $(a = 1)$, the only change in the national output deflator would be due to the change in the value of the price of the jth good from $\hat{p}_j$ to p_j. If $(\partial y/\partial a)$ has the same sign as $(p_j - \hat{p}_j)$, the effect of technological progress $(a > 1)$ is to magnify the effect of the change in p_j. In other words, the jth good receives increased weight in the index when $(\partial y/\partial a)$ and $(p_j - \hat{p}_j)$ agree in sign. That is, if $(\partial y/\partial a)$ and $(p_j - \hat{p}_j)$ agree in sign, the jth good ought to receive more weight in a national output index because of Hicks-neutral technological progress in the production of the first good. Similarly, if $(\partial y/\partial a)$ and $(p_j - \hat{p}_j)$ disagree in sign, then technological change reduces the effect of the change in p_j and the jth good ought to receive reduced weight.

For our purposes, a change in more than one price can be thought of as a series of individual price changes. Therefore, these conclusions are not restricted to cases in which only one price changes between the two periods.

Notice that a (weak) sufficient condition for $(\partial y/\partial a)$ and $(p_1 - \hat{p}_1)$ to share the same sign is that θ_{11} be nonnegative. Thus, if the supply curve ('money' value of output held constant) is not downward sloping, then technological progress reduces the weight of a change in p_1, and the first good ought to receive less weight in a national output index. It will turn out that this is guaranteed in the homothetic case.

If the PPM $\equiv \{(x_1, x_2, \ldots, x_r; \mu): \phi(x_1/a, x_2, \ldots, x_r) = \mu > 0\}$ is homothetic, then we know that the national output deflator $(y/\hat{y})$ is such that

$$\left(\frac{p'\hat{x}}{\hat{p}'\hat{x}}\right) \leq \left(\frac{y}{\hat{y}}\right) \leq \left(\frac{p'x}{\hat{p}'x}\right), \tag{7.15}$$

because the price indices on the left and the right do not account for substitution effects.[19] The price index on the right in (7.15) is the Paasche index (weighted by the vector of current outputs). If technology does not change $(a = 1)$, the price index on the left would be a Laspeyres index (weighted by the vector of base-period outputs). In the case of unchanging technology $\hat{x} = \tilde{x}$, where $\tilde{x}$ is an r-dimensional vector with the element $\tilde{x}_i$ denoting the quantity of the ith good $(i = 1, 2, \ldots, r)$ actually produced during the base period. Since the vector $\hat{x}$ is not observed while the vector $\tilde{x}$ is observed, it is important to know the relationship of the Laspeyres index $(p'\tilde{x}/\hat{p}'\tilde{x})$ to the unobserved price index $(p'\hat{x}/\hat{p}'\hat{x})$. This is the purpose of the following theorem, which of course also provides guidance as to the even more important question of the relationship of the Paasche index to the deflator based on yesterday's PPM.[20]

Theorem 7.3. $$\frac{\partial x_1}{\partial a} = \frac{\hat{x}_1}{a}(1+\theta_{11}), \quad \text{and}$$

$$\frac{\partial \hat{x}_i}{\partial a} = \frac{\hat{x}_i}{a}\theta_{i1} \quad \text{for } i = 1,2,...,r.$$

Proof. Theorem 7.3 can be easily proved after manipulation of equation (7.2). It is more interesting, however, to study the problem when the output of the first good is deflated by the technological parameter a. Let $\hat{x}_1^* \equiv \hat{x}_1/a$ be the amount of the first good produced (in deflated units) when prices are $\hat{p}$. $\hat{p}_1^* \equiv \hat{p}_1 a$ is the price per deflated unit of the first good. Equilibrium output of the various goods measured in deflated units depends only on prices per deflated unit and the 'money' value of output $\hat{y}$. Therefore we conclude that

$$\left(\frac{\partial \hat{x}_1^*}{\partial a}\right)\left(\frac{\partial a}{\partial \hat{p}_1^*}\right)_{\hat{p}_1 \text{ const.}} = \left(\frac{\partial \hat{x}_1^*}{\partial \hat{p}_1}\right)\left(\frac{\partial \hat{p}_1}{\partial \hat{p}_1^*}\right)_{a \text{ const.}} \tag{7.16}$$

and

$$\left(\frac{\partial \hat{x}_i}{\partial a}\right)\left(\frac{\partial a}{\partial \hat{p}_1^*}\right)_{\hat{p}_1 \text{ const.}} = \left(\frac{\partial \hat{x}_i}{\partial \hat{p}_1}\right)\left(\frac{\partial \hat{p}_1}{\partial \hat{p}_1^*}\right)_{a \text{ const.}}, \quad i = 2,...,r. \tag{7.17}$$

Using the definitions of $\hat{x}_1^*$, $\hat{p}_1^*$, and θ_{i1} in equations (7.16) and (7.17) completes the proof of the theorem. In Theorem 7.3, the gross supply elasticities ('money' value of output constant) θ_{i1} $(i=1,2,...,r)$ are evaluated at $\hat{p}$, $\hat{x}$, and $\hat{y}$.

If the PPM is homothetic, we can derive from Theorem 7.3 sufficient conditions for the observed Laspeyres price index to bound the national output deflator based on today's PPM from below. For example, if $\theta_{11} > -1$ and $\theta_{i1} > 0$ $(i = 2,...,r)$, then by Theorem 7.3, $\hat{x}_i > \tilde{x}_i$ $(i = 1,2,...,r)$ if there has been technological progress in the production of the first good $(a > 1)$. Then, if the price of the first good has risen, $p_1 > \hat{p}_1$, we have that $(p'\hat{x}/\hat{p}'\hat{x}) > (p'\tilde{x}/\hat{p}'\tilde{x})$. In this special case, therefore, the observed Laspeyres price index lies below the unobserved price index $(p'\hat{x}/\hat{p}'\hat{x})$. Further, if the PPM is homothetic, we have shown that in this special case the national output deflator must lie between the observed Laspeyres price index and the observed Paasche index,

$$\left(\frac{p'\tilde{x}}{\hat{p}'\tilde{x}}\right) \leqslant \left(\frac{y}{\hat{y}}\right) \leqslant \left(\frac{p'x}{\hat{p}'x}\right).$$

This result can also be deduced from Theorem 7.2, because $(\partial y/\partial a) > 0$ in this special case.

Theorem 7.3 reinforces Theorem 7.2. For example, Theorem 7.3 states that with $\theta_{11} > -1$, had the current technology $(a > 1)$ been in practice during the base period, output of the first good would have been higher. For the case $\theta_{i1} > 0$ $(i = 2, ..., r)$, had the current technology been in practice, output of the ith good $(i = 2, ..., r)$ would have been greater. Therefore, in constructing a Laspeyres price index, the first good should receive increased (decreased) weight if $\theta_{11} > -1$ $(\theta_{11} < -1)$. The ith good $(i = 2, ..., r)$ should receive more (less) weight if $\theta_{i1} > 0$ $(\theta_{i1} < 0)$. According to Theorem 7.2, similar changes must be made in the national output deflator. The Paasche price index retains its property as an upper bound on the deflator based on today's PPM (given homotheticity) without corrections.

Obviously, reversal of dates and of the movement in a yields parallel results as to the crucial relation between the Paasche price index and the deflator based on yesterday's PPM.

The case in which the PPM is homothetic is worthy of detailed analysis. This, of course, is the case in which in the absence of technological change the Laspeyres and Paasche price indices bound the national output deflator. More importantly, many leading descriptions of technology imply homotheticity of the PPM. For example, if each of the r production functions $g^i(\cdot)$ $(i = 1, 2, ..., r)$ in equation (7.1) exhibits constant returns, then the associated PPM is homothetic, and there are other cases as well. The purpose of the following theorem is to exploit the special information available when the PPM is homothetic. The results depend on the net supply elasticities η_{i1}, η_{1i}, and on the shares $\alpha_i = p_i x_i/y$.

Theorem 7.4. Assume that the PPM is homothetic.

(A) Suppose $p_i = \hat{p}_i$ for $i = 2, ..., r$. Then $(\partial y/\partial a)$ and $(p_1 - \hat{p}_1)$ share the same sign.

(B) Suppose $p_i = \hat{p}_i$ for $i = 1, 2, ..., r$ and $i \neq j$, $j \neq 1$. If $\eta_{j1} > \alpha_1$, then $(\partial y/\partial a)$ and $(p_j - \hat{p}_j)$ share the same sign. If $\alpha_1 > \eta_{j1}$, then $(\partial y/\partial a)$ and $(\hat{p}_j - p_j)$ share the same sign. If $\eta_{j1} = \alpha_1$, then $(\partial y/\partial a) = 0$.

(C) Suppose $p_i = \hat{p}_i$ for $i = 1, 2, ..., r$ and $i \neq j$, $j \neq 1$. If $\eta_{1j} > \alpha_j$, then $(\partial y/\partial a)$ and $(p_j - \hat{p}_j)$ share the same sign. If $\alpha_j > \eta_{1j}$, then $(\partial y/\partial a)$ and $(\hat{p}_j - p_j)$ share the same sign. If $\eta_{1j} = \alpha_j$, then $(\partial y/\partial a) = 0$.

Proof. (A) follows from Lemma 7.4. Note that the net supply elasticity η_{11} is always positive[21] while the share of output $0 < \alpha_1 < 1$. (B) and (C) also follow from Lemma 7.4 and definitions (7.11) and (7.13). Note here that $0 < \alpha_j < 1$.

For the interesting case in which the PPM is known to be homothetic, important practical implications follow. The good whose production has experienced Hicks-neutral technological progress (the first good) should receive more weight in a national output deflator based on today's PPM than in one based on yesterday's PPM. For $j \neq 1$, if the net supply elasticity η_{j1} is greater (less) than the first good's share of 'money' output α_1, then the jth good should receive more (less) weight. An equivalent statement is that if the net supply elasticity η_{1j} is greater (less) than the jth good's share of 'money' output α_j, then the jth good should receive more (less) weight.[22]

Theorems 7.2–7.4 yield sharp *qualitative* results. It may be of some interest to know how the effects described in these theorems vary with the size of the price change $(p_j - \hat{p}_j)$. It is therefore helpful to study the second-order partial derivative $(\partial^2 y / \partial a \, \partial p_j)$.

Lemma 7.5.
$$\frac{\partial^2 y}{\partial a \, \partial p_1} = \frac{1}{p_1}(\eta_{11} + 1)\left(\frac{\partial y}{\partial a}\right) + \hat{x}_1 \, \hat{\phi}_1 \left(\frac{p_1}{a x_1 \, \phi_1^2}\right)\left(\frac{\partial z}{\partial p_1}\right)$$

and

$$\frac{\partial^2 y}{\partial a \, \partial p_j} = \frac{1}{p_j}\eta_{j1}\left(\frac{\partial y}{\partial a}\right) + \hat{x}_1 \, \hat{\phi}_1 \left(\frac{p_1}{a x_1 \, \phi_1^2}\right)\left(\frac{\partial z}{\partial p_j}\right) \quad (i = 2, ..., r).$$

Proof. The lemma follows from Theorem 7.1, remembering that, by definition, $z(p) = x_1 \, \phi_1$.

Lemma 7.6. (A) Suppose $p_i = \hat{p}_i$ for $i = 2, ..., r$. For p_1 sufficiently close to $\hat{p}_1$,

$$\text{sign}\left(\frac{\partial^2 y}{\partial a \, \partial p_1}\right) = \text{sign}\left(\frac{\partial z}{\partial p_1}\right).$$

(B) Suppose $p_i = \hat{p}_i$ for $i \neq j$, $j = 2, ..., r$. For p_j sufficiently close to $\hat{p}_j$,

$$\text{sign}\left(\frac{\partial^2 y}{\partial a \, \partial p_j}\right) = \text{sign}\left(\frac{\partial z}{\partial p_j}\right) \quad (i = 2, ..., r).$$

Proof. This follows from Corollary 7.1 and Lemma 7.5.

Theorem 7.5. (A) Suppose $p_i = \hat{p}_i$ for $i = 2, ..., r$. For p_1 sufficiently close to $\hat{p}_1$,

$$\left(\frac{\partial^2 y}{\partial a\,\partial p_1}\right) \gtreqless 0 \text{ as } \theta_{11} \gtreqless -1.$$

Moreover, this holds for *all* $p_1 > \hat{p}_1$.

If the PPM is homothetic, then for *all* p_1,

$$\left(\frac{\partial^2 y}{\partial a\,\partial p_1}\right) > 0.$$

(B) Suppose $p_i = \hat{p}_i$ for $i \neq j$, $j = 2, ..., r$. For p_j sufficiently close to $\hat{p}_j$,

$$(\partial^2 y/\partial a\,\partial p_j) \gtreqless 0 \text{ as } \theta_{j1} \gtreqless 0 \quad (j = 2, ..., r).$$

If the PPM is homothetic, then for p_j sufficiently close to $\hat{p}_j$,

$$(\partial^2 y/\partial a\,\partial p_j) \gtreqless 0 \text{ as } \eta_{j1} > \alpha_1 \quad (j = 2, ..., r).$$

If the PPM is homothetic and p_j is in a sufficiently small neighborhood of $\hat{p}_j$, then it is also true that

$$(\partial^2 y/\partial a\,\partial p_j) \gtreqless 0 \text{ as } \eta_{1j} > \alpha_j \quad (j = 2, ..., r).$$

Furthermore, if $\eta_{j1} \geqslant 0$, then all the above statements hold for all $p_j > \hat{p}_j$. If $\eta_{j1} \leqslant 0$, then all the above statements hold for all $p_j < \hat{p}_j$.

Proof. The theorem follows from Theorems 7.2 and 7.4, Lemmas 7.1 and 7.4–7.6, and the fact that $\eta_{11} > 0$.

For at least these particular cases studied in Theorem 7.5, second-order effects reinforce first-order effects. The effects of technological change on proper weights in the national output deflator are larger for larger price changes.

VIII. *Changing Factor Supplies and*
Factor-Augmenting Technological Change: The Two-Sector Model
We now turn to the investigation of two formally equivalent cases: (1) that in which the relative supplies of factors change from period to period, and (2) that in which technological change is purely factor-augmenting and does not depend on the sector in which the factor is employed. For ease

of exposition and the sake of concreteness, much of the analysis is in terms
of the well-known two-sector model.[23]

In the next section, we generalize to the case of r outputs and m factors.
We then study the case in which the rate of factor-augmenting technological
change varies from sector to sector, and return again in Section 10 to the
two-sector model to obtain more detailed results.

We now outline the two-sector model.[24] In any period, the quantity of
(say) consumption goods Y_C produced depends on the respective quantities
of (say) capital K_C and labor L_C, devoted to that sector.

$$Y_C = F_C(K_C, L_C). \tag{8.1}$$

Similarly, the quantity of (say) investment goods produced Y_I is given by

$$Y_I = F_I(K_I, L_I), \tag{8.2}$$

where K_I and L_I are, respectively, the quantities of capital and labor devoted
to the I-sector. The consumption value of output Y is given by

$$Y = Y_C + pY_I, \tag{8.3}$$

where p is the consumption goods price of investment. If factors are fully
employed,

$$K_I + K_C = K, \quad L_I + L_C = L, \tag{8.4}$$

where K and L are, respectively, the amounts of capital and labor (completely inelastically) supplied in the period.

If factors are mobile and efficiently allocated, and if production is not
completely specialized, then

$$\frac{\partial F_C}{\partial L_C} = p\,\frac{\partial F_I}{\partial L_I} = w, \quad \frac{\partial F_C}{\partial K_C} = p\,\frac{\partial F_I}{\partial K_I} = r, \tag{8.5}$$

where w and r are, respectively, the competitive wage rate for labor and
the competitive rental rate on capital.

We now assume that there are constant returns-to-scale in production,
so that the analysis can proceed in terms of intensive units. We define

$$k = \frac{K}{L}, \quad y = \frac{Y}{L}$$

and

$$k_i = \frac{K_i}{L_i}, \quad y_i = \frac{Y_i}{L_i}, \quad l_i = \frac{L_i}{L}, \quad i = I, C$$

and

$$\omega = \frac{w}{r}.$$

The equations (8.1) and (8.2) can be rewritten as

$$y_i = l_i f_i(k_i), \quad i = I, C \tag{8.6}$$

where

$$f_i(k_i) = F_i(k_i, 1).$$

It is assumed that $f_i(\cdot)$ is twice continuously differentiable and that

$$f_i(k_i) > 0, \quad f_i'(k_i) > 0, \quad f_i''(k_i) < 0, \quad \text{for } 0 < k_i < \infty, \tag{8.7}$$

where primes denote differentiation.

Conditions (8.1) through (8.6) reduce to

$$\omega = \frac{f_i(k_i)}{f_i'(k_i)} - k_i, \quad i = I, C, \tag{8.8}$$

$$p = \frac{f_C'(k_C)}{f_I'(k_I)}, \tag{8.9}$$

$$y = y_C + p y_I, \tag{8.10}$$

$$y_I = f_I(k_I) \frac{k_C - k}{k_C - k_I}, \quad y_C = f_C(k_C) \frac{k - k_I}{k_C - k_I}. \tag{8.11}$$

Differentiation in (8.8) shows that k_i is uniquely determined by and is increasing in the wage–rental ratio ω,

$$\frac{dk_i}{d\omega} = \frac{-[f_i'(k_i)]^2}{f_i(k_i) f_i''(k_i)} > 0, \tag{8.12}$$

from (8.7). Capital intensities $k_i(\omega)$ are fundamental properties of the production functions given in (8.1) and (8.2), and they will play an important role in the following analysis. Before proceeding, we will present a basic result in two-sector comparative statics [see, for example, Rybczynski (1955) and Uzawa (1963)].

Lemma 8.1. $(dp/d\omega) \gtrless 0$ as $k_C(\omega) \gtrless k_I(\omega)$.

Proof. Logarithmic differentiation of (8.9) and substitution in (8.8) and (8.12) yield

$$\frac{1}{p}\frac{dp}{d\omega} = \frac{1}{k_1+\omega} - \frac{1}{k_C+\omega},$$

which shares the sign of $(k_C - k_1)$.

A remark about the special case with $k_C(\omega) = k_1(\omega)$ is in order. In this case, the PPF is a straight line segment; thus, there is one and only one price ratio p consistent with nonspecialized production. Therefore, analysis of nontrivial equal capital intensity cases will necessarily involve the study of specialized production.[25] If, on the other hand, $k_C(\omega) \neq k_1(\omega)$, then *along the* PPF, y_1 is a strictly concave function of y_C, so that there is a whole range of positive and finite price ratios that are consistent with nonspecialization of production.[26] For the remainder of this section, we assume $k_C(\omega) \neq k_1(\omega)$.

We now turn to the analysis of the two-sector production model in terms of the formalism developed in Section 6. The aggregate capital–labor ratio k determines the production curve in (y_C, y_1)-space. From Lemma 8.1, we know that the price ratio p uniquely determines the wage–rentals ratio ω. From (8.12), ω uniquely determines the capital intensities $k_C(\omega)$ and $k_1(\omega)$. Since we have assumed that the technology exhibits constant returns-to-scale, specification of k then determines the full PPM in (Y_C, Y_1)-space. The PPF is then determined by scale, that is by L or by $K (=kL)$.

We analyze the effect on the true national output deflator of a change in the overall capital–labor ratio k. Such a change may be thought of as due to investment (an increase in K) or as due to a change in the labor force (L), or as stemming from a factor-augmenting technological change in both sectors with the amount of augmentation the same in both sectors. In the last case, factors must be considered as measured in efficiency units.

Given the base-period price ratio $\hat{p}$ and the PPM based upon the current capital–labor ratio k, the problem is to minimize labor employment L subject to producing a consumption value of output $\hat{Y}$. The relevant Lagrangian is

$$\Lambda_1 = L - \hat{\lambda}\{L[y_C(k, \hat{p}) + \hat{p}y_1(k, \hat{p})] - \hat{Y}\}. \tag{8.13}$$

$\hat{\lambda}$ is a nonnegative Lagrange multiplier. y_i $(i = I, C)$ is uniquely determined by k and $\hat{p}$ from Lemma 8.1 and equations (8.11). If $\hat{L}$ is the solution to this constrained minimization problem, then the first-order condition yields

$$\hat{L} = \hat{\lambda}\hat{Y}, \tag{8.14}$$

so that $\hat{\lambda}$ can be interpreted as the marginal labor cost of expanding the consumption value of output when the capital–labor ratio is fixed at k, the price ratio is $\hat{p}$, and the consumption value of output is $\hat{Y}$.

By the Envelope Theorem,

$$\frac{\partial \hat{L}}{\partial k} = \frac{\partial \Lambda_1}{\partial k} = -\hat{\lambda}\hat{L}\hat{r}, \tag{8.15}$$

where $\hat{r} = f_c'[k_c(\omega)] = \hat{p}f_1'[k_1(\omega)]$ is the rental rate on capital when the price ratio is $\hat{p}$. $\hat{r}$ is the first-order increase in the consumption value of output per head due to an increase in k, *ceteris paribus*, when the price ratio is $\hat{p}$. Thus, $\hat{L}\hat{r}$ is the first-order increase in Y due to an increase in k, *ceteris paribus*. But, since $\hat{\lambda}$ is the marginal labor cost of output, (8.15) says that the first-order reduction in $\hat{L}$ due to an increase in k, *mutatis mutandis*, is equal to the first-order reduction in $\hat{L}$ due to an increase in k, *ceteris paribus*.

Given the current price ratio p, the problem is to maximize the consumption value of output, when labor is constrained to be equal to $\hat{L}$ (or capital input constrained to be equal to $k\hat{L}$). The Lagrangian expression is

$$\Lambda_2 = L[y_c(p,k) + py_1(p,k)] - \frac{1}{\lambda}(L - \hat{L}), \tag{8.16}$$

where $\lambda = L/Y = \hat{L}/Y$ is a nonnegative Lagrange multiplier, which is interpreted as the marginal labor cost of output when the price ratio is p and labor input is $\hat{L}$.

By the Envelope Theorem, $\partial Y/\partial k = \partial \Lambda_2/\partial k$, so that

$$\frac{\partial Y}{\partial k} = Lr + \left(\frac{1}{\lambda}\right)\left(\frac{\partial \hat{L}}{\partial k}\right), \tag{8.17}$$

$$\frac{\partial Y}{\partial k} = Lr\left(1 - \frac{\hat{r}y}{r\hat{y}}\right), \tag{8.18}$$

where $\hat{y} = y_c(\hat{p},k) + \hat{p}y_1(\hat{p},k)$.

An alternate form of this result is

$$\frac{\partial Y}{\partial k} = \hat{L}\hat{r}\left(\frac{r}{\hat{r}} - \frac{y}{\hat{y}}\right), \tag{8.18'}$$

using the fact that in (8.16), L is constrained to equal $\hat{L}$. We shall comment on this form in the next section. In the present two-sector context, it is more convenient to observe that, by Walras' law, $y = rk + w$ and $\hat{y} = \hat{r}k + \hat{w}$, so (8.18) reduces to

$$\frac{\partial Y}{\partial k} = Lr\left(1 - \frac{\omega + k}{\hat{\omega} + k}\right). \tag{8.19}$$

Theorem 8.1. If $k_C > k_I$, then $\text{sign}(\partial Y/\partial k) = \text{sign}(\hat{p} - p)$. If, on the other hand, $k_I > k_C$, then $\text{sign}(\partial Y/\partial k) = \text{sign}(p - \hat{p})$.

Proof. The theorem follows from combining equation (8.19) with Lemma 8.1.

Corollary 8.1. If $p = \hat{p}$, then $(\partial Y/\partial k) = 0$.

Proof. The corollary follows immediately from equation (8.19) and the fact that the price ratio uniquely determines the wage–rentals ratio.

Theorem 8.1 and Corollary 8.1 are *global* results (that is, they hold for all values of p and $\hat{p}$) as long as capital intensities do not cross.[27]

Theorem 8.1 and Corollary 8.1 have important practical implications. Let the 'money' price of the investment good be p_I, the 'money' price of the consumption good be p_C, $p_I/p_C = p$. If the effective capital–labor ratio (in efficiency units) is unchanged from base period to current period, then the only change in true national output would be due to a change in either p_I or p_C. The change in the true national output deflator due to a change in p_i $(i = I, C)$ would be in the same direction as the change in p. If k (in efficiency units) is increasing through time, then the good whose production is more (less) capital intensive should receive increased (decreased) weight in the construction of the true national output deflator.[28]

It should be stressed that the analysis of this section applies to any two-sector model in which relative factor supplies change from period to period and in which technological change is purely factor augmenting at the same rate in each sector. Then, k must be interpreted as the ratio (in efficiency units) of the quantity of the first factor to the quantity of the second factor. y_C and y_I are then, respectively, the ratio of the quantity produced of the first good to the aggregate supply of the second factor and the ratio of the quantity produced of the second good to the aggregate supply of the second factor.

IX. *Changing Factor Supplies and*

Factor-Augmenting Technological Change: The General Case

In this section, we generalize the results of the preceding section to the many-sector model and consider, as far as possible, the case in which the production function for a single good exhibits factor-augmenting technological change at a rate *not* identical with that exhibited by the production functions for other goods. The price we pay for such generality, however, is fairly substantial. In the case in which a factor increases in supply (or has the same rate of augmentation in all sectors), we are able to generalize the preceding results through equation (8.18) or (8.18') and to give an economic interpretation to that result. As one might expect, however, the strong result of Theorem 8.1 seems to have no simple extension to the multisector case, although factor intensities clearly play an important role. In the case of factor-augmenting change in just one sector, the latter problem becomes even harder, although rather natural generalizations of all the other results to this case are readily available.

We begin, then, with the case in which there is no technological change, but the supply of some factor, say the *m*th, increases. (As already noted, this is equivalent to assuming that every sector experiences an *m*th-factor-augmenting technological change at the same rate.) Unfortunately, whereas in the case of a Hicks-neutral technological change an easy parametrization of the resulting shift in the PPM was available, that is not the case here and we must work with the underlying production functions.

Those production functions are denoted, as before, by

$$x_i = g^i(v_{i1}, ..., v_{im}) \quad (i = 1, ..., r) \tag{9.1}$$

where x_i is the amount of the *i*th good produced and v_{ij} is the amount of the *j*th factor used in its production.

The constraints on the system are given by

$$\sum_{i=1}^{r} v_{ij} = v_j; \quad v_{ij} \geq 0 \quad (i = 1, ..., r; j = 1, ..., m) \tag{9.2}$$

where the v_j denote the total amount of the *j*th factor used. The PPM is generated by considering those outputs (x_i) which can be produced when the v_j are given by

$$v_j = \mu v_j^0 \quad (j = 1, ..., m) \tag{9.3}$$

where v_j^0 is the amount of the jth factor available and μ (the factor 'dosage') is allowed to vary over positive scalars.

We are going to investigate the effect on the national output deflator of a change in v_m^0. The deflator itself is formally constructed from the production system and constraints (9.1)–(9.3), instead of directly from the PPM as in Section 6, as follows.

First, given base-period prices $\hat{p}$ and base-period value of production $\hat{y}$, we find the minimum μ for which $\hat{y}$ could be produced. Then, given that μ, which we shall call $\hat{\mu}$, we maximize value of production at current-period prices p. The resulting value y divided by the base-period value $\hat{y}$ is the index.

Accordingly, we must first set up the Lagrangian corresponding to the minimization of μ, given the base-period value. This is most easily accomplished by minimizing the ratio of v_1 to v_1^0 (the choice of which factor to use is arbitrary), while constraining all ratios of v_j to v_j^0 to be the same. Obviously, the common value of such ratios is μ. The appropriate Lagrangian is therefore

$$\Lambda_1 = \frac{\sum\limits_{i=1}^{r} v_{i1}}{v_1^0} + \sum_{j=2}^{m} \eta_j \left[\frac{\sum\limits_{i=1}^{r} v_{ij}}{v_j^0} - \frac{\sum\limits_{i=1}^{r} v_{i1}}{v_1^0} \right] - \lambda(\hat{p}'\hat{x} - \hat{y}), \qquad (9.4)$$

where λ and the η_j are Lagrangian multipliers.

If we call the resulting minimized value of μ, $\hat{\mu}$, the Lagrangian for the maximization of y is considerably simpler:

$$\Lambda_2 = p'x - \sum_{j=1}^{m} \pi_j \left(\sum_{i=1}^{r} v_{ij} - \hat{\mu} v_j^0 \right), \qquad (9.5)$$

the π_j being Lagrangian multipliers.

By applying the Envelope Theorem to (9.5), we obtain

$$\frac{\partial y}{\partial v_m^0} = \frac{\partial \Lambda_2}{\partial v_m^0} = \pi_m \hat{\mu} + \left(\frac{\partial \hat{\mu}}{\partial v_m^0} \right) \sum_{j=1}^{m} \pi_j v_j^0. \qquad (9.6)$$

To evaluate $(\partial \hat{\mu}/\partial v_m^0)$, we apply the Envelope Theorem again, this time to (9.4), obtaining

$$\frac{\partial \hat{\mu}}{\partial v_m^0} = \frac{\partial \Lambda_1}{\partial v_m^0} = \frac{-\eta_m \sum\limits_{i=1}^{r} v_{im}}{(v_m^0)^2} = \frac{-\eta_m \hat{\mu}}{v_m^0}, \qquad (9.7)$$

where the last equality follows from the definition of $\hat{\mu}$. Substituting (9.7) into (9.6), we obtain

Lemma 9.1. $\dfrac{\partial y}{\partial v_m^0} = \pi_m \hat{\mu} - \left(\dfrac{\eta_m \hat{\mu}}{v_m^0}\right) \displaystyle\sum_{j=1}^{r} \pi_j v_j^0 .$

We now proceed to simplify and interpret this result. In so doing, it will be convenient to assume constant returns, so that total factor payments equal total value of production. We shall assume constant returns for the remainder of this and the next section. (If constant returns are not assumed, our results still go through, but with factor wages interpreted as shadow wages and total values y and $\hat{y}$ interpreted as total factor payments at shadow wages.)

Lemma 9.2. $y = \hat{\mu} \displaystyle\sum_{j=1}^{r} \pi_j v_j^0 .$

Proof. Differentiating (9.5) with respect to any v_{ij} and setting the result equal to zero yields, as part of the first-order conditions for a maximum,

$$p_i \left(\frac{\partial g^i}{\partial v_{ij}}\right) = \pi_j \quad (i = 1, ..., r; \; j = 1, ..., m), \tag{9.8}$$

whence it is clear that π_j is the wage of the jth factor in the second period. Since the total amount of the jth factor employed in that period is ($\hat{\mu} v_j^0$), the lemma follows immediately from the constant-returns assumption.

Denote the wage of the jth factor in the second period by w_j and its wage in the base period by $\hat{w}_j$. Then, as just remarked, $w_j = \pi_j$. We now seek an expression for $\hat{w}_j$.

Lemma 9.3. Denoting the wage of the jth factor in the base period by $\hat{w}_j$, we have

$$\hat{w}_1 = \frac{1 - \displaystyle\sum_{j=2}^{m} \eta_j}{\lambda v_1^0}, \quad \hat{w}_j = \frac{\eta_j}{\lambda v_j^0} \quad (j = 2, ..., m).$$

Proof. Differentiating (9.4) with respect to any v_{ij} and setting the result equal to zero yields, as part of the first-order conditions for a maximum,

$$p_i \left(\frac{\partial g^i}{\partial v_{i1}}\right) = \frac{1 - \displaystyle\sum_{j=2}^{m} \eta_j}{\lambda v_1^0} \quad (i = 1, ..., r) \tag{9.9}$$

and

$$p_i\left(\frac{\partial g^i}{\partial v_{ij}}\right) = \frac{\eta_j}{\lambda v_j^0} \quad (i = 1, ..., r; \; j = 2, ..., m), \tag{9.10}$$

which is equivalent to the lemma.

Lemma 9.4. $\lambda = \hat{\mu}/\hat{y}$.

Proof. By constant returns, $\hat{y}$ equals total factor payments in the base period. The total amount of the jth factor employed in that period is $\hat{\mu}v_j^0$, so that Lemma 9.3 yields

$$\hat{y} = \sum_{j=1}^{m} \hat{w}_j(\hat{\mu}v_j^0) = \left(\frac{\hat{\mu}}{\lambda}\right)\left(1 - \sum_{j=2}^{m} \eta_j + \sum_{j=2}^{m} \eta_j\right) = \frac{\hat{\mu}}{\lambda}, \tag{9.11}$$

proving the lemma.

It is now easy to prove

Theorem 9.1. $\dfrac{\partial y}{\partial v_m^0} = \hat{\mu}\hat{w}_m\left(\dfrac{w_m}{\hat{w}_m} - \dfrac{y}{\hat{y}}\right).$

Proof. Combining Lemmas 9.1 and 9.2 and using the fact that $\pi_m = w_m$ yields

$$\frac{\partial y}{\partial v_m^0} = w_m\hat{\mu} - \frac{\eta_m}{v_m^0}y. \tag{9.12}$$

Application of Lemma 9.3 and then Lemma 9.4 shows

$$\frac{\eta_m}{v_m^0} = \lambda\hat{w}_m = \frac{\hat{\mu}\hat{w}_m}{\hat{y}}. \tag{9.13}$$

Substituting (9.13) into (9.12) and rearranging yields the statement of the theorem.

Before interpreting Theorem 9.1, we note that it is the generalization of equation (8.18′) to the present case. The two expressions differ only in notation and in the way in which the problem is stated. Thus, in deriving (8.18′), we were concerned with the effects of an increase in the capital–labor ratio, which may be interpreted as an increase in capital, given labor. The return to capital appears in (8.18′) in precisely the same way as the return to the changing factor (the mth) appears in the theorem. The remaining difference is the appearance in (8.18′) of $\hat{L}$ in place of $\hat{\mu}$, which reflects the fact that in the two-sector model, we were able to avoid the complicated constraints involved in (9.4). In that model, we could in effect choose convenient units by taking the reference amount of labor available (the equivalent of v_1^0) to be unity, thus making $L = \hat{\mu}$.

Corollary 8.1 also carries over immediately to the present case:

Corollary 9.1. If $p = h\hat{p}$ for some scalar $h > 0$, then $(\partial y / \partial v_m^0) = 0$.

Proof. It is obvious that if $p = h\hat{p}$, then $w_m = h\hat{w}_m$ and $y = h\hat{y}$.

The corollary is obvious in any case, since if all prices are multiplied by h, the national output deflator will be equal to h regardless of what PPM is used.

We can now proceed to interpret Theorem 9.1. To do so, it will be convenient to define $\beta_m = (w_m v_m / y)$ and $\hat{\beta}_m = (\hat{w}_m v_m / \hat{y})$ as the shares of the mth factor in the current and base periods, respectively.[29] Then Theorem 9.1 can be restated as

Theorem 9.1'. $\dfrac{\partial y}{\partial v_m^0} = \left(\dfrac{y}{v_m^0}\right)(\beta_m - \hat{\beta}_m)$,

from which it is clear that what matters is whether the share of the mth factor goes up or down as a result of the price change. That is: *If, with prices p, the share of the mth factor is greater (less) than with prices $\hat{p}$, the effect of an increase in the supply of that factor will be to increase (decrease) the national output deflator when the new rather than the old PPM is used.*

The case of a proportional price change, covered in Corollary 9.1, is of course a case in which the price change leaves all factor shares unaltered.

What does this mean in terms of the relative importance of the various goods in the deflator before and after the price change? We can best investigate this by examining cases in which p differs from $\hat{p}$ in only one component.

Theorem 9.2. If a rise in the price of the kth good ($k = 1, \ldots, r$) would increase (decrease) the share of the mth factor, then an increase in the supply of the mth factor leads to an increase (decrease) in the relative importance of the kth price in the national output deflator.

Proof. First, suppose that all prices except the kth remain the same but that the kth price rises; that is, $p_i = \hat{p}_i$, $i = 1, \ldots, r$, $k \neq i$, and $p_k > \hat{p}_k$. Then, with either PPM, $y > \hat{y}$ and the deflator will exceed unity. If the rise in the ith price leads to an increase in the share of the mth factor, then by Theorem

9.1', the effect of a rise in the supply of the mth factor will be to increase the deflator. On the other hand, suppose that with all other prices constant, $p_k < \hat{p}_k$. Then with either PPM, $y < \hat{y}$, and the deflator will be less than unity. However, the decrease in p_k will, by assumption, decrease the share of the mth factor, so that Theorem 9.1' shows that an increase in the supply of that factor will decrease the deflator in this situation. Thus, if increases in the price of the kth good increase the share of the mth factor, the effect of an increased supply of that factor will be to magnify the effect of the kth price on the deflator. Similarly, it is clear that if an increase in the kth price *decreases* the share of the mth factor, then an increase in the supply of that factor will diminish the effect of changes in the kth price on the deflator.

It may be remarked that this result is global rather than local, in the sense that it holds over any region of price and factor supply changes in which the indicated relationships remain valid.

Further insight into Theorem 9.2 can be gained by considering the way in which a Laspeyres price index would have to be changed to reflect the conditions prevailing with the new PPM (or, equivalently, the way in which a Paasche price index would have to be changed to reflect the conditions prevailing with the old PPM). We shall prove a theorem reinforcing Theorem 9.2 in precisely the same way that Theorem 7.3 reinforces Theorem 7.2, and shall show that had the mth factor supply been greater in the initial period, the production of the kth good would have been greater (less) relative to total income y if and only if a rise in the price of that good would have increased (decreased) the share of the mth factor.

To do this directly would require examination of the way in which $\hat{\beta}_m$ varies with $\hat{p}_k$ and $(\hat{x}_k/\hat{y})$ varies with v_m^0, when the maximizing problem is that whose Lagrangian is given by (9.4). This is moderately inconvenient, however, and the presence of constant returns makes it just as acceptable to work with (9.5) and to examine the variation of β_m with p_k and of (x_k/y) with v_m^0. We first prove a lemma reflecting the duality between factor supplies and outputs on the one hand and wages and prices on the other.

Lemma 9.5. $\dfrac{\partial x_k}{\partial(\hat{\mu} v_m^0)} = \dfrac{\partial w_m}{\partial p_k}$ $(k = 1, ..., r)$.

Proof. By the Envelope Theorem applied to (9.5),

$$\frac{\partial y}{\partial p_k} = \frac{\partial \Lambda_2}{\partial p_k} = x_k \tag{9.14}$$

and

$$\frac{\partial y}{\partial(\hat{\mu}v_m^0)} = \frac{\partial \Lambda_2}{\partial(\hat{\mu}v_m^0)} = \pi_m = w_m. \tag{9.15}$$

(Note that $\partial y/\partial v_m^0$ as evaluated here and in the proof of Theorem 9.3 later is not the same as that evaluated in Theorem 9.1, because only one optimization problem is involved here.) Thus

$$\frac{\partial x_k}{\partial(\hat{\mu}v_m^0)} = \frac{\partial^2 y}{\partial p_k \partial(\hat{\mu}v_m^0)} = \frac{\partial w_m}{\partial p_k}, \tag{9.16}$$

and the lemma is proved.

Lemma 9.5 can also be proved through direct calculation of the derivatives involved.

With this result in hand, it is now easy to prove

Theorem 9.3. $\dfrac{\partial \beta_m}{\partial p_k} = v_m^0 \dfrac{\partial(x_k/y)}{\partial v_m^0}.$

Proof.

$$\frac{\partial(x_k/y)}{\partial v_m^0} = \frac{y(\partial x_k/\partial v_m^0) - x_k(\partial y/\partial v_m^0)}{y^2} = \frac{\hat{\mu}[y(\partial w_m/\partial p_k) - x_k w_m]}{y^2}, \tag{9.17}$$

by Lemma 9.5, the Envelope Theorem applied to (9.5), and the fact that $\pi_m = w_m$. On the other hand,

$$\frac{\partial \beta_m}{\partial p_k} = \frac{\hat{\mu}v_m^0[y(\partial w_m/\partial p_k) - w_m(\partial y/\partial p_k)]}{y^2} = \frac{\hat{\mu}v_m^0[y(\partial w_m/\partial p_k) - w_m x_k]}{y^2}, \tag{9.18}$$

by the Envelope Theorem applied, as before, to (9.5). Comparison of (9.17) and (9.18) yields the statement of the theorem.

The meaning of the theorem in relation to Theorem 9.2 has already been discussed. Before moving on, we might observe that the asymmetrical appearance of v_m^0 in the theorem is due to working with the share of the *m*th factor, rather than with the ratio of w_m to y, the variable most directly analogous to the ratio of x_k to y. It is obvious from Theorem 9.1 (rather than Theorem 9.1′) that this would have suited our purposes equally well, although perhaps it would have seemed less natural.

Returning to the main thread of our discussion, Theorem 9.2, as already indicated, is the parallel of Theorem 7.2 in the present case. Note that whereas in Theorem 7.2 we were concerned with the effect of essentially an output-augmenting technological change in the PPM, the present case can be considered that of a factor-augmenting technological change. It is interesting that where in the earlier case (see Theorem 7.4) we found the results to turn on the share of the outputs, in the present case we find that the shares of the factors are involved, although this seems to exhaust the extent of the symmetry.

Unfortunately, Theorem 9.2 is about as far as it seems possible to go in the direction of generalizing the two-sector model's Theorem 8.1 to the multisector case. The problem, of course, is that in the present context, unlike the two-sector one, it is not at all straightforward to derive more basic conditions under which a rise in the price of the kth good will lead to an increase in the share of the mth factor. Indeed, this is an old and well-known problem in the analysis of factor price equalization in international trade.[30]

Some idea of the difficulties involved can be obtained by specializing to the case in which $r = m$, so that there are exactly as many factors as commodities. Let F be the factor-intensity matrix; that is,

$$F = \begin{bmatrix} v_{11}/x_1 & \cdots & v_{1r}/x_1 \\ \cdot & & \cdot \\ \cdot & & \cdot \\ \cdot & & \cdot \\ v_{r1}/x_r & \cdots & v_{rr}/x_r \end{bmatrix}. \tag{9.19}$$

Let w denote the r-component column vector of factor wages and p (as before) the r-component column vector of prices. Then, from constant returns, it is clear that at all points of equilibrium

$$p = Fw \tag{9.20}$$

or

$$w = F^{-1}p, \tag{9.21}$$

assuming (for simplicity) that F is nonsingular. It follows that to trace the effect of a change in p_k on β_m requires knowledge of the inverse of the factor-intensity matrix (and how the change in prices affects it). Whereas in the two-sector case, it is possible to state conditions on the factor intensities which determine the signs of the elements of that inverse, no similar simple conditions are known for the more general r-sector case (let alone for the case in which $r \neq m$). Which is in part to say that there is no general definition of relative factor intensity for the case with $r > 2$.

We have thus gone as far as seems possible in the analysis of the present problem. It is clear that the determination in practice of the effect of a change in factor supply on the national output deflator and the measurement of national output itself requires considerably more detailed information than was the case with a Hicks-neutral change, considered in Section 7, where what was required was knowledge of supply elasticities and output shares.

We now turn to a case more general than that so far considered in this section, and find (not suprisingly) that while rather natural generalizations of the results so far obtained can be readily proved, the results seem further from practical usefulness than those just considered.

As was mentioned several times, the case of an increase in the supply of the mth factor can be equivalently considered as a case of mth-factor-augmenting technological change proceeding at the same rate in every production function. We now take up the problem of the analysis of the effects on the national output deflator of an mth-factor-augmenting technological change in a *single* production function; the case of such changes proceeding at different rates in different production functions is readily derived from this.

Accordingly, we keep the production functions for goods $2, ..., r$ (we now return to the general case of $r \neq m$) as before, but alter the production function of the first good to be

$$x_1 = g^1(v_{11}, ..., v_{1m-1}, bv_{1m}) \qquad (9.22)$$

where $b > 0$ is a parameter, an upward shift in which represents an mth-factor-augmenting technological change in the production of the first good. We begin by finding $\partial y/\partial b$.

To do this, we must distinguish between two notations. We shall let g^1_m denote the partial derivative of g^1 with respect to its mth argument, while letting $\partial g^1/\partial v_{1m}$ continue to denote the partial derivative of g^1 with respect to v_{1m} itself. Thus, $\partial g^1/\partial v_{1m} = bg^1_m$. Moreover, it will be important to distinguish between v_{1m}, the amount of the mth factor employed in the production of the first good when (9.5) is involved (the second period) and $\hat{v}_{1m}$, the corresponding employment when (9.4) is involved (the first period). We shall denote with carets derivatives evaluated at the solution of the first-period problem.

Define

$$\beta_{1m} = \frac{w_m v_{1m}}{y}, \quad \hat{\beta}_{1m} = \frac{\hat{w}_m \hat{v}_{1m}}{\hat{y}}, \qquad (9.23)$$

so that β_{1m} is the share in current national output of the mth factor employed in the production of the first good, and similarly for $\hat{\beta}_{1m}$. We prove the following generalization of Theorem 9.1′.

Theorem 9.4. $\dfrac{\partial y}{\partial b} = \left(\dfrac{y}{b}\right)(\beta_{1m} - \hat{\beta}_{1m}).$

Proof. Applying the Envelope Theorem to (9.5), we obtain

$$\frac{\partial y}{\partial b} = \frac{\partial \Lambda_2}{\partial b} = p_1 g_m^1 v_{1m} + \left(\sum_{j=1}^{m} \pi_j v_j^0\right)\left(\frac{\partial \hat{\mu}}{\partial b}\right) = \frac{w_m v_{1m}}{b} + \frac{y}{\hat{\mu}}\left(\frac{\partial \hat{\mu}}{\partial b}\right),$$

$$(9.24)$$

where the final equality follows from the first-order conditions and Lemma 9.2. Applying the Envelope Theorem to (9.4) yields

$$\frac{\partial \hat{\mu}}{\partial b} = \frac{\partial \Lambda_1}{\partial b} = -\lambda \hat{p}_1 \hat{g}_m^1 \hat{v}_{1m} = -\lambda \frac{\hat{w}_m \hat{v}_{1m}}{b} = \frac{-\hat{\mu}\hat{w}_m \hat{v}_{1m}}{b\hat{y}}, \qquad (9.25)$$

where the final equality follows from the first-order conditions and Lemma 9.4. Substitution of (9.25) into (9.24) yields the statement of the theorem.

We have called Theorem 9.4 a generalization of Theorem 9.1′, and so it is. Suppose that instead of an mth-factor-augmenting change in only the first production function, we had such a change in *every* production function, with the parameter of such a change in the ith production function denoted by b_i. Obviously, Theorem 9.4 gives the effects on y of changes in any of the b_i, with obvious notational changes. Now suppose that for some subset of commodities, say, $1, \ldots, h$, with $h \leqslant r$, all the b_i were identical and identically equal to b. Then Theorem 9.4 would yield as an immediate corollary

Corollary 9.2. If production functions $1, \ldots, h$ experience mth-factor-augmenting technological change at a common rate, the common parameter being denoted by b, then

$$\frac{\partial y}{\partial b} = \left(\frac{y}{b}\right)\left(\sum_{i=1}^{h} \beta_{im} - \sum_{i=1}^{h} \hat{\beta}_{im}\right). \qquad (9.26)$$

In particular, if $h = r$, so that the change is common to all production functions,

$$\frac{\partial y}{\partial b} = \left(\frac{y}{b}\right)(\beta_m - \hat{\beta}_m). \qquad (9.27)$$

Proof. This is an immediate consequence of Theorem 9.4 (with appropriate notational changes), the fact that $b_i = b$ $(i = 1, ..., h)$, and

$$\frac{\partial y}{\partial b} = \sum_{i=1}^{h} \left(\frac{\partial y}{\partial b_i}\right)\left(\frac{\partial b_i}{\partial b}\right). \tag{9.28}$$

The final statement of Corollary 9.2 can be seen to be identical with Theorem 9.1′, if we recall that in that theorem what is being varied is v_m^0. If we examined the derivative of y with respect to the total amount of the mth factor available $(\hat{\mu}v_m^0)$, the factor (y/v_m^0) in the statement of Theorem 9.1′ would be replaced by $(y/\hat{\mu}v_m^0)$. Similarly, in the case of Corollary 9.2, the *effective* total supply of the mth factor is $(b\hat{\mu}v_m^0)$. If we evaluated the derivative of y with respect to this rather than with respect to b, then the factor (y/b) in (9.27) would be replaced by $(y/b\hat{\mu}v_m^0)$, or one over the share of an *efficiency unit* of the mth factor.

We now return to the case of an mth-factor-augmenting technological change which occurs only in the production of the first commodity. It is clear that the generalization of Theorem 9.2 is

Theorem 9.5. If a rise in the price of the kth good $(k = 1, ..., r)$ (other prices constant) would increase (decrease) the share in total output of that part of the mth factor employed in the production of the first good (and thus that part directly affected by the technological change), then the mth-factor-augmenting technological change in the production of the first commodity leads to an increase (decrease) in the relative importance of the kth price in the national output deflator.

The proof is essentially the same as that of Theorem 9.2.

We can also derive a result generalizing Theorem 9.3 and bearing the same relation to Theorem 9.5 as Theorem 9.3 does to Theorem 9.2. As in deriving Theorem 9.3, it is convenient and also sufficient to work with the maximizing problem whose Lagrangian is given by (9.5). We first replace Lemma 9.5 with

Lemma 9.6. $\dfrac{\partial x_k}{\partial b} = \dfrac{v_{1m}}{b}\dfrac{\partial w_m}{\partial p_k} + \dfrac{w_m}{b}\dfrac{\partial v_{1m}}{\partial p_k}$ $(k = 1, ..., r)$.

Proof. By the Envelope Theorem applied to (9.5),

$$\frac{\partial y}{\partial p_k} = x_k \tag{9.29}$$

and

$$\frac{\partial y}{\partial b} = p_1 v_{1m} g_m^1 = \frac{v_{1m} p_1 (\partial g^1 / \partial v_{1m})}{b} = \frac{w_m v_{1m}}{b}, \qquad (9.30)^{31}$$

using the first-order conditions and the fact that $\pi_m = w_m$. Thus

$$\frac{\partial x_k}{\partial b} = \frac{\partial^2 y}{\partial p_k \partial b} = \frac{\partial (w_m v_{1m}/b)}{\partial p_k}, \qquad (9.31)$$

proving the lemma.

Lemma 9.6, like Lemma 9.5, can also be proved by direct (and relatively laborious) calculation of the derivatives involved.

It is now easy to prove

Theorem 9.6. $\dfrac{\partial \beta_{1m}}{\partial p_k} = b \dfrac{\partial (x_k/y)}{\partial b}$ $(k = 1, \dots, r)$.

Proof.

$$\frac{\partial \beta_{1m}}{\partial p_k} = \frac{y \left(v_{1m} \dfrac{\partial w_m}{\partial p_k} + w_m \dfrac{\partial v_{1m}}{\partial p_k} \right) - w_m v_{1m} \dfrac{\partial y}{\partial p_k}}{y^2} = \frac{by \dfrac{\partial x_k}{\partial b} - w_m v_{1m} x_k}{y^2}$$

$$(9.32)$$

by Lemma 9.6 and the Envelope Theorem applied to (9.5). On the other hand,

$$\frac{\partial \left(\dfrac{x_k}{y} \right)}{\partial b} = \frac{y \dfrac{\partial x_k}{\partial b} - x_k \dfrac{\partial y}{\partial b}}{y^2} = \frac{y \dfrac{\partial x_k}{\partial b} - x_k p_1 v_{1m} g_m^1}{y^2} = \frac{y \dfrac{\partial x_k}{\partial b} - \dfrac{x_k v_{1m} w_m}{b}}{y^2}$$

$$(9.33)$$

by the Envelope Theorem applied to (9.5) and the first-order conditions. Comparison of (9.32) and (9.33) yields the statement of the theorem.

Unfortunately, while Theorems 9.4–9.6 may seem elegant and illuminating, they are even farther from being of practical use than are Theorems 9.1–9.3, which they generalize. In order to apply Theorem 9.5, for example, information is required not merely on the share of the mth factor and how it varies with particular prices (as would be required for Theorem 9.2), but on the share of that portion of the mth factor employed in the production of a particular output (the first). At best, this is no easier to obtain than the information required to apply the less general theorem.

This concludes our study of factor-augmenting change in the general multisector model, but more can be said about the special two-sector case to which we now return.

x. Factor-Augmenting Technological Change in a Single Sector of the Two-Sector Model

Earlier we were able to exploit the simplicity of the two-sector production model in deriving specific results for the case where technological change is purely factor augmenting at the same rate in each sector. We are now interested in the case of factor-augmenting technological change with differing rates of augmentation in the various sectors. Again, we turn to the two-sector model[32] for concreteness.

For example, assume that only labor employed in the C-sector is subject to labor-augmenting technological change. If b is the technological parameter, then

$$Y_C = F_C(K_C, bL_C), \tag{10.1}$$

$$Y_I = F_I(K_I, L_I), \tag{10.2}$$

and

$$Y = Y_C + pY_I. \tag{10.3}$$

If factors are fully employed,

$$K_C + K_I = K \tag{10.4}$$

and

$$L_C + L_I = L. \tag{10.5}$$

Define $X_C \equiv bL_C$, labor in efficiency units employed in the C-sector. If factors are fully mobile and efficiently allocated between sectors, then

$$\frac{\partial Y_C}{\partial K_C} = p \frac{\partial Y_I}{\partial K_I} = r \tag{10.6}$$

and

$$\frac{\partial Y_C}{\partial L_C} = b \frac{\partial Y_C}{\partial X_C} = p \frac{\partial Y_I}{\partial L_I} = w, \tag{10.7}$$

where w is the wage rate and r the rentals rate.

Given the base-period price ratio $\hat{p}$ and the PPM defined by the current endowments K and L, we analyze the effect on the national output deflator of a change in b.

Lemma 10.1. $\dfrac{\partial Y}{\partial b} = \dfrac{Y}{b}\left(\dfrac{wL_C}{Y} - \dfrac{\hat{w}\hat{L}_C}{\hat{Y}}\right)$. Furthermore, $\left(\dfrac{\partial y}{\partial b}\right) = 0$ when $p = \hat{p}$.

Proof. The lemma follows from Theorem 9.4 and the fact that when $p = \hat{p}$, we know that $w = \hat{w}$, $L_C = \hat{L}_C$, and $Y = \hat{Y}$.

Next we define $z(p)$ by

$$z(p) = \frac{wL_C}{Y}. \tag{10.8}$$

In order to study the effects of price changes on $z(p)$, we logarithmically differentiate in (10.8), obtaining

$$\frac{1}{z}\frac{\partial z}{\partial p} = \frac{1}{w}\frac{\partial w}{\partial p} + \frac{1}{L_C}\frac{\partial L_C}{\partial p} - \frac{1}{Y}\frac{\partial Y}{\partial p}. \tag{10.9}$$

We proceed to analyze the right-hand side of (10.9), term by term.

Lemma 10.2. Let $\beta_K = rK/Y$ be capital's share of national income and $\beta_L = wL/Y = 1 - \beta_K$ be labor's share. Then

$$\frac{1}{Y}\frac{\partial Y}{\partial p} = \frac{\beta_K}{r}\frac{\partial r}{\partial p} + \frac{\beta_L}{w}\frac{\partial w}{\partial p}.$$

Proof. By Euler's Theorem

$$Y = rK + wL. \tag{10.10}$$

The lemma follows from differentiating (10.10) and substituting β_K and β_L in the result.

Lemma 10.3. Let $\sigma_j = (\omega/k_j)(\partial k_j/\partial\omega)$ be the elasticity of factor substitution in sector j $(j = I, C)$.[33] Then

$$\frac{\partial L_C}{\partial p} = \frac{-(K_C\sigma_C + K_I\sigma_I)}{\omega(k_C - k_I)}\frac{\partial\omega}{\partial p} < 0.$$

Proof. Holding K, L, and b fixed and differentiating the full-employment conditions yields

$$\frac{\partial K_C}{\partial p} + \frac{\partial K_I}{\partial p} = 0 \tag{10.11}$$

and

$$\frac{\partial L_C}{\partial p} + \frac{\partial L_I}{\partial p} = 0. \tag{10.12}$$

From the definition of the elasticity of substitution σ_j, we have that

$$\frac{1}{K_j}\frac{\partial K_j}{\partial p} - \frac{1}{L_j}\frac{\partial L_j}{\partial p} = \frac{\sigma_j}{\omega}\frac{\partial \omega}{\partial p}, \tag{10.13}$$

for $j = I, C$. Substituting from (10.11) and (10.12) in (10.13) and rearranging yields the system

$$\begin{bmatrix} k_C & k_I \\ 1 & 1 \end{bmatrix} \begin{bmatrix} \dfrac{\partial L_C}{\partial p} \\ \dfrac{\partial L_I}{\partial p} \end{bmatrix} = \frac{-1}{\omega}\frac{\partial \omega}{\partial p} \begin{bmatrix} K_C \sigma_C + K_I \sigma_I \\ 0 \end{bmatrix}. \tag{10.14}$$

The lemma follows after solving (10.14) by Cramer's rule and noting that by Lemma 8.1 $\operatorname{sign}(\partial\omega/\partial p) = \operatorname{sign}(k_C - k_I)$.

Lemma 10.4.

$$\frac{1}{z}\frac{\partial z}{\partial p} = \left(\frac{1}{\omega}\frac{\partial \omega}{\partial p}\right)\left[\beta_K - \frac{K_C \sigma_C + K_I \sigma_I}{L_C(k_C - k_I)}\right].$$

Proof. Substituting the results of Lemmas 10.2 and 10.3 in equation (10.9) yields

$$\frac{1}{z}\frac{\partial z}{\partial p} = \left[\frac{K_C \sigma_C + K_I \sigma_I}{-\omega(k_C - k_I)L_C}\right]\left(\frac{\partial \omega}{\partial p}\right) - \left(\frac{\beta_K}{r}\frac{\partial r}{\partial p} + \frac{\beta_L}{w}\frac{\partial w}{\partial p}\right) + \frac{1}{w}\frac{\partial w}{\partial p}. \tag{10.15}$$

Substituting $(1 - \beta_K)$ for β_L in (10.15) and noting that $(1/\omega)(\partial\omega/\partial p) = (1/w)(\partial w/\partial p) - (1/r)(\partial r/\partial p)$ establishes the lemma.

Lemma 10.5. If $k_I > k_C$, then $\partial z/\partial p < 0$.

Proof. In this case by Lemma 8.1, $\partial\omega/\partial p < 0$. Noting that when $k_I > k_C$ the term in brackets in the statement of Lemma 10.4 is positive completes the proof.

Lemma 10.6. If $\sigma_I \geqslant 1$ and $\sigma_C \geqslant 1$, then $\partial z/\partial p < 0$.

Proof. By Lemma 10.5 we need only study the case in which $k_C > k_I$. (We have excluded the case $k_C = k_I$, since this necessarily involves study of complete specialization, that is, corner solutions in production.) Then the term in brackets on the RHS of the statement of Lemma 10.4 is not larger than

$$\frac{rK}{Y} - \frac{K}{L_C(k_C - k_I)} \tag{10.16}$$

since $\beta_K = rK/Y$ and by hypothesis $K_C \sigma_C + K_I \sigma_I \geqslant K$. Expression (10.16) is equal to

$$\frac{K[rK_C - Y - rK_I L_C/L_I]}{Y L_C (k_C - k_I)} < 0 \tag{10.17}$$

since $Y > rK_C$.

In the next lemma, we weaken the hypothesis of Lemma 10.6.

Lemma 10.7. If $\sigma_C \geqslant 1$, then $\partial z/\partial p < 0$.

Proof. Again Lemma 10.5 allows us to restrict our attention to the case where $k_C > k_I$. First, we employ two standard results (see, for example, Uzawa, 1963) of two-sector theory:

$$\frac{\partial Y_C}{\partial p} < 0 \tag{10.18}$$

and

$$\frac{\partial Y}{\partial p} > 0. \tag{10.19}$$

[The validity of (10.18) and (10.19) is easily established by drawing a national income line with slope $(-p)$ tangent to the (strictly convex) PPF in the $Y_I - Y_C$ plane.] Combining (10.18) and (10.19) yields

$$\frac{\partial (Y_C/Y)}{\partial p} < 0. \tag{10.20}$$

Define $\alpha(p)$, the fraction of C-sector income paid in wages, $\alpha(p) = wL_C/Y_C$. (It should be remarked that when $\sigma_C = 1$, labor's share of sector-C income is constant; that is $\alpha(p)$ is independent of p.) From Lemma 8.1, when $k_C > k_I$, $(\partial \omega/\partial p) > 0$.

Now, by Euler's Theorem,

$$Y_C = rK_C + wL_C \tag{10.21}$$

so that

$$\frac{1}{\alpha(p)} = \frac{Y_C}{wL_C} = \frac{k_C}{\omega} + 1. \tag{10.22}$$

When $\sigma_C \geqslant 1$, that is, when $\partial k_C/\partial \omega \geqslant k_C/\omega$, $\partial \alpha/\partial \omega \leqslant 0$, whence $\partial \alpha/\partial p \leqslant 0$ also (by Lemma 8.1). Since $Y/Y_C \equiv z/\alpha$, Lemma 10.7 follows from this and (10.20).

Theorem 10.1. In the two-sector model with labor-augmenting techno-logical change in the C-sector

$$\text{sign}\left(\frac{\partial Y}{\partial b}\right) = \text{sign}(\hat{p}-p)$$

if either (A) the I-sector is the more capital-intensive sector ($k_1 > k_C$) or (B) the C-sector elasticity of factor substitution is not less than unity ($\sigma_C \geqslant 1$).

Proof. The theorem follows after applying the results of Lemmas 10.5 and 10.7 in Lemma 10.1.

Corollary 10.1. If either (A) the I-sector is the more capital-intensive sector ($k_1 > k_C$) or (B) the C-sector elasticity of factor substitution is not less than unity ($\sigma_C \geqslant 1$), then the effect of a labor-augmenting technological change in the C-sector is to decrease the relative importance of the price of the investment good in the national output deflator.

Moreover, as we know, this corresponds to

Corollary 10.2. If either (A) or (B) of Theorem 10.1 and Corollary 10.1 holds, $\partial(Y_1/Y)/\partial b < 0$.

Proof. This follows from Theorem 9.6 and Lemmas 10.5 and 10.7.

We now return to the multisector case.

XI. *General Technological Change*

It may be worthwhile providing a brief generalization of some of the results of previous sections to the case of a general technological change in the production function of the first commodity.[34] Naturally, we shall not be able to obtain particular results of practical usefulness as long as we maintain a high level of generality, but such a treatment may usefully show what was special and what general about the cases so far considered.

Accordingly, we leave the production functions for goods $2, ..., r$ as before, but alter the production function of the first good to be

$$x_1 = g^1(v_{11}, ..., v_{1m}; b) \tag{11.1}$$

where b is a technological change parameter.[35] We shall denote $\partial g^1/\partial b$ by g_b^1, and, as with other derivatives, shall denote with a caret its value at base-period values of the arguments.

We continue to assume constant returns and prove

Theorem 11.1. $\dfrac{\partial y}{\partial b} = \hat{p}_1 \hat{g}_b^1 \left(\dfrac{p_1 g_b^1}{\hat{p}_1 \hat{g}_b^1} - \dfrac{y}{\hat{y}} \right).$

Proof. Applying the Envelope Theorem to (9.5), we obtain

$$\frac{\partial y}{\partial b} = \frac{\partial \Lambda_2}{\partial b} = p_1 g_b^1 + \left(\sum_{j=1}^{m} \pi_j v_j^0 \right) \left(\frac{\partial \hat{\mu}}{\partial b} \right) = p_1 g_b^1 + \left(\frac{y}{\hat{\mu}} \right) \left(\frac{\partial \hat{\mu}}{\partial b} \right),$$

(11.2)

where the final equality follows from Lemma 9.2. Applying the Envelope Theorem to (9.4) yields

$$\frac{\partial \hat{\mu}}{\partial b} = \frac{\partial \Lambda_1}{\partial b} = -\lambda \hat{p}_1 \hat{g}_b^1 = -\frac{\hat{\mu} \hat{p}_1 \hat{g}_b^1}{\hat{y}},$$

(11.3)

where the final equality follows from Lemma 9.4. Substituting from (11.3) into (11.2) and rearranging yields the statement of the theorem.

It is clear that $p_1 g_b^1$ is the first-order marginal effect on the value of output of the technological change—the marginal revenue product of the technological change, as it were. By an argument identical to that of the proof of Theorem 9.2, Theorem 11.1 is readily seen to imply

Theorem 11.2. If a rise in the price of the kth good ($k = 1, ..., r$) (other prices constant) would increase (decrease) the ratio of the marginal revenue product of technological change to the total value of output, then the technological change leads to an increase (decrease) in the importance of the kth price in the national output deflator.

We can also derive a result which bears the same relation to Theorem 11.2 as Theorem 9.3 does to Theorem 9.2, or Theorem 9.6 to Theorem 9.5, or for that matter, Theorem 7.3 to Theorem 7.2. As in the previous section, it is convenient and also sufficient to work with the maximizing problem whose Lagrangian is given in (9.5). We first prove

Lemma 11.1. $\dfrac{\partial x_k}{\partial b} = \dfrac{\partial (p_1 g_b^1)}{\partial p_k}$ ($k = 1, ..., r$).

Proof. By the Envelope Theorem applied to (9.5) we obtain

$$\frac{\partial y}{\partial p_k} = x_k$$

(11.4)

and

$$\frac{\partial y}{\partial b} = p_1 g_b^1.$$ (11.5)[36]

Thus

$$\frac{\partial x_k}{\partial b} = \frac{\partial^2 y}{\partial p_k \partial b} = \frac{\partial (p_1 g_b^1)}{\partial p_k},$$ (11.6)

and the lemma is proved.

It is now easy to prove

Theorem 11.3. $\dfrac{\partial (p_1 g_b^1/y)}{\partial p_k} = \dfrac{\partial (x_k/y)}{\partial b}$ $(k = 1, ..., r).$

Proof.

$$\frac{\partial \left(\dfrac{p_1 g_b^1}{y}\right)}{\partial p_k} = \frac{y \dfrac{\partial (p_1 g_b^1)}{\partial p_k} - (p_1 g_b^1) \dfrac{\partial y}{\partial p_k}}{y^2} = \frac{\dfrac{\partial (p_1 g_b^1)}{\partial p_k} - p_1 g_b^1 x_k}{y^2},$$ (11.7)

by the Envelope Theorem applied to (9.5). Similarly,

$$\frac{\partial \left(\dfrac{x_k}{y}\right)}{\partial b} = \frac{y \dfrac{\partial x_k}{\partial b} - x_k \dfrac{\partial y}{\partial b}}{y^2} = \frac{y \dfrac{\partial x_k}{\partial b} - x_k p_1 g_b^1}{y^2}.$$ (11.8)

The desired result now follows immediately from Lemma 11.1.

Thus, an increase in the kth price will increase the marginal revenue product of a technological change relative to total money output if and only if, with prices constant, the effect of the technological change will be to increase production of the kth commodity, relative to total money output. This obviously reinforces Theorem 11.2.

XII. *New Goods, Disappearing Goods, and Corner Solutions*
So far we have been assuming that a positive amount of every good is produced in every period. It is obviously important to remove this assumption and to deal with the possibility of corner solutions. Clearly, the market basket of goods produced in the economy does not always contain the same items; new goods are produced and old ones disappear. The question thus naturally arises as to how the prices of such goods ought to be treated in national output deflation.

In the case of new goods, unlike what is ordinarily true of disappearing goods, there are two subcases to consider. The first of these is that which naturally comes to mind when thinking of a new good—the case of a new invention, of a good which is now produced for the first time because in earlier years the technology for producing it did not exist in some sense. Actually, this is only a limiting case. Most new goods could have been produced at times before they actually were; technical improvements in their manufacture were required to bring the cost down to a profitable level, but earlier production would have been possible at a higher price. This kind of new good introduction shares with that of a pure new invention the property that the good has appeared for the first time as a result of a change in the PPM.

The second kind of new good is one which could perfectly well have been produced earlier, but which was not produced because consumers would not have bought it at a profitable price. Because of a taste change, that is no longer so and the good now appears for the first time because of changes in tastes rather than in the PPM. It is clear that this is also often the case of a disappearing good with the two periods reversed.

Real cases may often be some admixture of these two polar ones, but study of the pure cases will allow us to treat mixed ones. We shall refer to a new good which appears with no taste change but only because of a change in the PPM as a new good for reasons of *supply*. Similarly, we shall refer to a good which appears with an unchanging PPM because of a taste change as a new good for reasons of *demand*. We may note that the case of goods which are new for reasons of supply was essentially the only case treated in our study of the cost-of-living index (Essay I); since this is the case which ordinarily comes to mind, this was perhaps not too great an oversight, particularly as we shall show that the conclusion reached is essentially the same. The isomorphic case for the national output deflator, however, turns out to be that of goods which are new for reasons of demand, and it would obviously be inappropriate to treat only this. We shall, in fact, treat both cases and, as a natural by-product, easily extend the treatment of the cost-of-living index to cover goods which are new for reasons of demand.

We begin, however, by analyzing the national output deflator when there is a good which is new for reasons of demand. (As already mentioned, this is the case which is isomorphic both to that treated in Essay I and to the case of a disappearing good.) Here the PPM is unchanged, but some good, say the first, was not produced in the base period because no one wanted to buy it, at least not at prices which would have made it profitable to produce. Thus, in the base period, the point of actual production lies in the inter-section of the PPF with the hyperplane defined by $\hat{x}_1 = 0$. There is no actual price quotation for the first commodity in the first period.

The lack of such a quotation is not a major problem for the national output deflator, which can be found (in principle) without reference to the missing price. It is somewhat more convenient (and more in line with general practice), however, to consider such a price explicitly.

In Section 6, we began by locating the crucial value of μ by solving the problem:

$$\text{Minimize } \mu \text{ subject to } \hat{p}'\hat{x} = \hat{y}. \tag{12.1}$$

In the present case, there is no observed value for $\hat{p}_1$. It will obviously suffice to set $\hat{p}_1 = 0$, or indeed, to set it at any price sufficiently low to ensure that $\hat{x}_1$ will be zero when the minimization problem is solved. All such values for $\hat{p}_1$ will lead to the same result. The highest of such prices is what we shall term the *supply reservation price*; it is the intercept on the (properly interpreted) supply curve for the first commodity.[37]

It is less arbitrary in some sense, however, not to proceed in this way and to replace (12.1) by

$$\text{Minimize } \mu \text{ subject to } \hat{p}'\hat{x} = \hat{y} \text{ and } \hat{x}_1 = 0. \tag{12.1'}$$

This obviously leads to the same result.

Note that, with an appropriate adjustment of units, the supply reservation price is the shadow price of the constraint $\hat{x}_1 = 0$. That shadow price is the amount of resource 'dose' μ which would just need to be used up to produce one unit of the first commodity. The supply reservation price of the first commodity gives the same quantity in terms of dollars—the price at which the product of one unit of the first commodity would just be worth the value of the resources devoted to it.

With either of these treatments, then, the lack of a price quotation for the first commodity in the base period is not a problem for the construction of the national output deflator when the first commodity is new for reasons of demand. Neither is this a problem for the construction of a Laspeyres price index in which that commodity will receive zero weight in any case.

It is obviously a problem, however, for the construction of a Paasche price index. (Note that the cases would be reversed for a disappearing good.) We now turn to that problem.

We saw in Section 4 that a Paasche deflator bounds the true national output deflator from above when the present problem is not encountered.[38] Obviously, we want to preserve that property. It is not hard to show that this will be accomplished if, in the construction of the Paasche deflator, we use for $\hat{p}_1$ any price at or below the supply reservation price.

To see this, observe that in both the Paasche deflator and the national output deflator which it bounds (the one using today's PPM and PPF), the numerator will be the same, namely, the value of today's output at current prices $p'x$. Given a choice of $\hat{p}_1$, the denominator of the Paasche deflator will be simply $\hat{p}'x$, while the denominator of the national output deflator, essentially as we have seen,[39] will be the largest value of output that could have been obtained with prices $\hat{p}$, on the same PPF as x, and with zero production of the first commodity. If $\hat{p}_1$ is set at or below the supply reservation price, however, the constraint that the first commodity not be produced will not be binding, so the denominator of the national output deflator is the unconstrained maximum value which could have been achieved at prices $\hat{p}$ on the same PPF as x. It is obvious that this is not less than $\hat{p}'x$ and that it will be greater if the PPF is strictly convex.

This obviously leads to the conclusion that *the value used for $\hat{p}_1$ in the construction of the Paasche index should be the supply reservation price or below*, just as in the parallel case for the cost-of-living index, a similar argument leads to the use of a price at the demand reservation price or above. Moreover, since of all Paasche indices which bound the national output deflator from above, it is obviously desirable to use the one providing the least upper bound, we see immediately that the proper price to use in this situation is the supply reservation price itself, just as we found in the parallel case for the cost-of-living index that the proper price to use was the demand reservation price itself. This is a natural result in the light of the shadow price interpretation of the supply reservation price.

Note that the supply reservation price here involved is the one with factor supplies fixed and the remaining prices fixed at their base-period values. In the case of a disappearing good, the remaining prices would be fixed at their current-period values.

We now turn to the case of a good which is new for reasons of supply.

Here the problem is somewhat different. In the case of a good which is new for reasons of demand, the construction of the national output deflator could proceed by restricting $\hat{x}_1$ to be zero because that was a case in which there was no demand for the first commodity at profitable prices. Obviously the same thing is true here when we consider the national output deflator based on *yesterday's* PPM; no really new problem arises when that is the deflator to be used, and we have already suggested that it is the more appropriate of the two deflators. The numerator of the deflator based on yesterday's PPM is, as before, the maximum value that could have been produced by the economy with yesterday's resources at today's prices. If the first good could have been produced yesterday at today's prices, such production will properly enter the numerator; if the first good was a pure new invention (or would have a very high supply reservation price at today's prices), then in that maximum, x_1 will be zero and the entire money value of production of the first good will be treated as a contribution to real output, other things equal. In either case, the correct procedure is clear.

When we consider the national output deflator based on today's PPM, however, the matter is a bit more complicated. (Note that it is this deflator which is bounded by a Paasche index.) In constructing this deflator, we must maximize the value of production which would have been achieved with today's PPF at yesterday's prices. In the pure case of a good new for reasons of demand, we could do this constraining the production of the first good to be zero, considering that no demand for the good existed at profitable prices. In the present case, such a procedure might well be inappropriate. Had we had today's technology and yesterday's demand conditions, it is entirely possible that the first good would have been produced and sold. A price quotation for that good might perfectly well have existed and been higher than the supply reservation price. All we can say in this case is that such a price would certainly not have been higher than the *demand* reservation price, or else the good would not have been produced essentially for reasons of demand. To put it another way, it is possible that with today's technology the first good could have been profitably sold yesterday. Such sales would have been profitable if they could have been made above the supply reservation price and they would have been nonzero had they been made below the demand reservation price. What in fact the price would have been, we do not know without examination of the general equilibrium of all markets.

Fortunately, such ambiguity does not prevent us from reaching a definite conclusion as to what price should be used in the construction of the Paasche deflator. There are two cases to consider.

First, suppose that the demand reservation price for the good in question would have lain above the supply reservation price. Then the good would have been produced and the national output deflator should use the price at which it would have been produced—some price in the interval between the two reservation prices. A Paasche deflator which used the same price as the national output deflator would certainly be one, as we know, which bounded the latter deflator from above. *A fortiori*, a Paasche deflator which uses the (in this case) lower supply reservation price will certainly also bound the national output deflator from above.

The second case is that in which the demand reservation price would still have lain below the supply reservation price. In this case, the first good would not have been produced yesterday even with today's technology, and the restriction that the first good would not have been produced will be an appropriate one in the construction of the national output deflator. Indeed, we are now back in the case of a good new for reasons of demand, despite the change in the PPM, and our previous analysis applies. The supply reservation price should be used in the construction of the Paasche deflator. (Note that this time it is the supply reservation price which would have been obtained with *today's* PPM.)

Thus in every case we find that the supply reservation price should be used in the construction of a Paasche deflator. Only in the case of a good wholly new for reasons of supply (in the sense that it could have been profitably produced *and sold* last period had current technology and resources been available) does this fail to put the most efficient upper bound on the national output deflator. Even in this case, such use does provide an upper bound; discovery of the most efficient upper bound, like discovery of the value of the national output deflator itself, would require knowledge of the price at which transactions would actually have taken place.

Before closing, we may briefly extend our earlier treatment of new goods in the cost-of-living index to cover goods new for reasons of *demand*. This is the case in which, had today's tastes ruled yesterday, the first good, say, would have been produced and *bought*. That transaction would have taken place at a price below the demand reservation price (but above the supply reservation price), and the true cost-of-living index ought to be calculated using that price. Since, in practice, the correct price will be unknown, the best we can do is to use a Paasche cost-of-living index which provides a lower bound on the true one, and we shall certainly achieve this by using a Paasche index which employs the demand reservation price.[40] So in any case, the demand reservation price should be used, although only in the case of a good new for reasons of supply will it provide the most efficient lower bound on the true cost-of-living index.

XIII. *Quality Changes*

In this section, we take up the question of how quality change in one of the goods ought properly to be treated in the construction of the national output deflator. This is a difficult problem, largely because it is so difficult to model quality changes in an adequate way, and we are unable to reach any positive recommendation. All that we are actually able to do is to show the circumstances in which a treatment of quality change along fairly standard lines will in fact be appropriate. Not too suprisingly, those circumstances turn out to be quite restrictive.

Suppose that there is a quality change in the first good. The old variety of the good (for simplicity) ceases to be produced and a new one is instead. Obviously, in principle, this can be treated as a combination of the disappearance of an old good and the appearance of a new one; in practice, this is not done and it would be cumbersome to do so. We continue to treat automobiles today as in some sense the same commodity as automobiles of a few years ago, even though there are many differences of greater or less importance. It is clear that one may wish to make an adjustment to the national output deflator in order to take such quality changes into account. Assuming, for the sake of definiteness, that the new quality of the good is somehow an improvement over the old one, then, in the case of the cost-of-living index, if prices have not changed one wants to say that the cost-of-living has gone down because consumers are better off being able to buy the new variety than they would have been had they only been able to purchase the old one.

Similarly, in the present case, even if all outputs, as measured, are unchanged, we may wish to regard real output as having risen because the new variety of good may embody more resources than did the old one. To put it differently, with the same resources and technology, had the old variety been produced, other outputs and all prices remaining fixed, it is possible that more of it would have been produced than was produced of the new variety. In such a case, we would not want the shift from the old to the new variety to disguise the fact that the capacity of the economy to produce real output has increased. If more steel, labor, and other inputs are embodied in new cars than in old ones, then the production of a given number of cars represents a bigger output when new cars are involved than when old ones are. Moreover, this is true regardless of how consumers view the change. Their views and tastes are relevant for deciding whether the cost of living has decreased and their real *income* risen, but not for deciding whether real output in terms of the production system has risen (except insofar as tastes affect prices).

Accordingly, in such a case, we would want to reduce the national output deflator so that an unchanged money output will correspond to an increased real output. It is natural to seek to do this by a downward adjustment in the price of automobiles.

Formally, let b be a parameter indexing the quality change. Given $\hat{y}, \hat{p}$, and p, y, the numerator of the national output deflator will depend on b. Since $\hat{y}$ and $\hat{p}$ will remain fixed throughout this discussion, we may suppress them and write $y = y(p_1, ..., p_r, b)$. Taking a value of b equal to unity for the case of no quality change, adjustment of the price of the first commodity to take account of the effects of the quality change amounts to finding a p_1^* such that

$$y(p_1^* \, p_2, ..., p_r, 1) = y(p_1, p_2, ..., p_r, b). \tag{13.1}$$

In general, it will be possible to find such a p_1^*. The problem arises when we require (as is natural to do in practice) that the appropriate price adjustment be made knowing only the physical characteristics of the good involved (here summarized by b) and possibly the amount of its production, or in general, knowing only the production functions for the new and old qualities of the good. One would expect to use this information to determine, as it were, the relative quantities of resources embodied in each quality. Ordinarily such adjustments would not be allowed to depend, in particular, on the outputs of the other commodities not affected by the quality change. Unfortunately, such a natural-appearing requirement leads to very restrictive conditions on the kinds of changes in resource use which quality changes so treated can represent.

Since the problem is fully isomorphic to that treated in Section 5 of

Essay I for the case of quality adjustments to the cost-of-living index, we shall simply state and interpret the crucial result without repeating the proof. It is

Theorem 13.1. (A) A necessary and sufficient condition for p_1^* to be independent of $x_2, ..., x_r$ is that the shift in the PPF resulting from the quality change be representable as

$$\hat{\mu} = \phi(g^*(x_1, b) x_1, x_2, ..., x_r).$$ (13.2)

(B) If, in addition, p_1^* is to be independent of x_1, or if there are everywhere constant returns, then the function $g^*(x_1, b)$ is independent of x_1 and the shift in the PPF can be represented as

$$\hat{\mu} = \phi(bx_1, x_2, ..., x_r)$$ (13.3)

by an appropriate choice of units for b. In the constant-returns case, this will be true of the entire PPM, and not merely of the PPF corresponding to $\hat{\mu}$.

If we write $b = 1/a$ and compare (13.3) with the discussion at the beginning of Section 7, we see immediately that the condition of the theorem is that, from the point of view of resource use, the shift from the old to the new quality of the good must appear as equivalent to a Hicks-neutral technological change in the production function of the first good.[41] If constant returns are not imposed and the price adjustment is allowed to depend on the amount of the first commodity produced, then the extent of the Hicks-neutral change can also depend on the amount of that production, but it will be Hicks-neutral, nevertheless. *The new variety must embody more of every kind of factor than the old variety and the percentage change in factor usage must be the same for all factors.*[42] This is obviously an extremely restrictive condition.

Unfortunately, this rather negative conclusion is as far as we have been able to take the analysis. What adjustments should be made in the case of more general and realistic quality changes remains to be studied.[43]

FOOTNOTES FOR ESSAY II

[1] Ignoring aggregation and other difficulties. See, for example, Samuelson (1947); v. Hofsten (1952); Fisher and Shell (1968) (Essay I).

[2] For earlier attempts along these lines see Bergson (1961, pp. 25–41) and Moorsteen (1961).

[3] This is not an innocuous assumption and we shall have to deal with it later.

[4] This is natural only if some efficiency assumptions are made about production. If there is not perfect competition or if, for any reason, resources are underutilized, production will generally not be on the PPF. Since output indices and deflators have to be constructed even in imperfect worlds, we discuss these problems later but assume them absent for the time being.

[5] Of course, we are not the first to do so. See, for example, Richter (1966).

[6] It is a basic source of the lack of independence of path observed by Richter (1966).

[7] It should be noted that, apart from the two sets of indices under discussion, two additional ones can be similarly constructed. This corresponds to the fact that even with an unchanged PPM there would be two indices. Thus, one might construct an index in the following way. Consider the PPM obtaining when x^C was produced. To compare y^A and y^C using that PPM, we might begin by finding the PPF tangent to the price line through x^A which has slope corresponding to p^A. In general, the tangency will *not* occur at x^A. Starting with this PPF, consider what money output would have been had prices been p^B. Call that money output $y^{B'}$. Then the movement from y^A to $y^{B'}$ could be considered purely a price movement and that from $y^{B'}$ to y^C a real output change. Similarly, an index could be constructed using the PPM which obtained when x^A was produced and finding the PPF tangent to the price line through x^C corresponding to prices p^B.

These two indices do not seem to us to be of much direct interest (although the reader is free to differ). Unlike the two indices with which we have been concerned, these new ones employ a PPF which never existed. On the other hand, if the PPM's are homothetic, then the new indices will be the same as the old ones and we shall want to make use of this property.

[8] Naturally, alternative policies will generally lead to alternative prices. This is largely beside the point, however. The focus of real output indices is to take tastes as given and reflected through fixed demand prices, just as the focus of cost-of-living indices is to take production possibilities as given and reflected through fixed supply prices.

[9] The situation is the same (but the result as to which map should be used different) in the case of a cost-of-living index when tastes change. See Essay I. In both cases, it is the relevance of current tastes that matters.

[10] This comes about, of course, because in one case value is maximized subject to a production constraint concave to the origin while in the other, cost is minimized subject to an indifference curve constraint which is convex to the origin. The price line is a separating hyperplane for the two relevant convex sets.

[11] The possibility that there is a contradiction and that we have shown that a Paasche index lies above a Laspeyres index which also lies above it is not a real one. Aside from the fact that cost-of-living and real output indices are not defined over the same commodities (which is not a valid answer to such an objection), prices can only change if either indifference maps or the PPM change. But if prices do not change, all these indices coincide and if either the PPM or indifference map changes, one of the inequalities ceases to be established.

[12] It is therefore not strictly correct to say that the published indices have an inflationary bias as compared with the relevant theoretically based index.

[13] In that analysis, we begin with a point of tangency to a given value line. We could certainly take that value line to correspond to $y^{A'}$ instead of to y^A; the value of $y^{A'}$, however, itself depends on the PPM, and the change in that value resulting from a change in the PPM would have to be ignored were we to follow this procedure. If the PPM is homothetic, however, the deflator using the PPF tangent to the value line corresponding to $y^{A'}$ will be identical with that using the PPF tangent to the value line corresponding to y^A, the preferred alternative in the text.

[14] It should be remarked, however, that the relation of Paasche and Laspeyres indices to our national output deflator, analyzed in the preceding section, breaks down in the case of market imperfections. This is because the point of actual production will lie outside the PPF we construct tangent to the actual value line. Hence the argument which shows the maximum value at the new prices achievable on the frontier to be greater than the value of the old output at the new prices breaks down. Similarly, difficulties arise for any choice of PPF for use in constructing the deflator. In our view, this is a serious difficulty for the interpretation of Paasche and Laspeyres indices in real situations.

[15] Note that only homotheticity of the second map need be assumed. This apparent asymmetry is only apparent. If the first map is homothetic, we could begin by redefining $\hat{y}$ to be the value which the second economy would actually have produced at prices $\hat{p}$. Everything would then go through as before.

[16] As already suggested, the formal description just given is entirely isomorphic to the description of the cost-of-living index. This can be

seen by changing minima to maxima and the reverse, and considering x as a vector of outputs, $\phi(x)$ as a utility function, and y as money income. (In the case of the cost-of-living index, homotheticity is not a particularly appealing assumption; on the other hand, in that case, separate interest does attach to a comparison based on a given budget constraint.)

[17] We assume unless otherwise stated that solutions to first-order conditions are interior. Corner solutions are discussed in Section 12.

[18] This fact follows, as it must, from the symmetry of the substitution terms. Thus

$$(\eta_{i1} - \alpha_1)\frac{\alpha_i}{\alpha_1} = \left\{\left(\frac{\partial x_i}{\partial p_1}\right)_{\phi=\hat{\mu}\,\text{const.}}\frac{p_1}{x_i} - \frac{p_1 x_1}{y}\right\}\frac{p_i x_i}{p_1 x_1}$$

$$= \left\{\left(\frac{\partial x_1}{\partial p_i}\right)_{\phi=\hat{\mu}\,\text{const.}}\frac{p_i}{x_1} - \frac{p_i x_i}{y}\right\} = \eta_{1i} - \alpha_i.$$

[19] See the discussion in Section 4. The inequalities are strict in the usual case where equal factor-dosage loci in $(x_1, x_2, ..., x_r)$-space are *strictly* concave to the origin and p is not a multiple of $\hat{p}$.

[20] See Section 4. We have chosen to work directly with the Laspeyres index and the deflator based on today's P P M so as not to burden the notation.

[21] It is an own substitution elasticity differing only in sign from the similar term in consumer theory.

[22] These statements are equivalent, by the remarks following Lemma 7.4.

[23] In order to avoid confusion, we will adopt the widely accepted notation and terminology of Uzawa's (1963) article. Although our references usually will be to Uzawa (1963), many of the comparative statics theorems appeared first in Rybczynski (1955). We are indebted to Winston W. Chang for helpful suggestions on applications of two-sector theory.

[24] In adopting the notation of Uzawa (1963), we introduce some contradiction with our earlier notation, but no confusion should arise.

[25] We treat "corner" cases in Section 12.

[26] The assertions in this paragraph are formally proved in Rybczynski (1955) and Uzawa (1963).

[27] Capital intensities are said to cross if there exist $\omega^{\dagger}$ and $\omega^{\dagger\dagger}$ such that $k_C(\omega^{\dagger}) > k_1(\omega^{\dagger})$ while $k_1(\omega^{\dagger\dagger}) > k_C(\omega^{\dagger\dagger})$.

[28] Because $\text{sign}(\partial Y/\partial k) = \text{sign}\left[(k_C - k_1)\left(\frac{\hat{p}_1}{\hat{p}_C} - \frac{p_1}{p_C}\right)\right]$.

[29] Note that the amount of the mth factor is $v_m = \hat{\mu} v_m^0$ in both periods.

[30] See, for example, Samuelson (1947). We are indebted to Pranab Bardhan for pointing this out to us.

[31] Note that $\partial y/\partial b$ as evaluated here and in the proof of Theorem 9.6 later is not the same as that evaluated in Theorem 9.4 because only one optimization problem is involved here.

[32] Except for the technological parameter b, our notation agrees with that of Uzawa (1963) and our Section 8.

[33] Recall that $k_j \equiv K_j/L_j$ and $\omega \equiv w/r$.

[34] Actually, an identical development applies to any change in the PPM, but changes induced by shifts in factor supplies have already been considered.

[35] Note that g^1 is now a function of $m+1$ variables.

[36] Note that $\partial y/\partial b$ as evaluated here and in the proof of Theorem 11.3 later is not the same as that evaluated in Theorem 11.1, because only one optimization problem is involved here.

[37] The supply curve in question is not the usual one with factor prices constant. It is the curve which shows how much of the first commodity would be produced as a function of its price, given fixed prices for the remaining commodities and also given fixed factor *supplies*.

[38] In that section, we observed that the deflator which was bounded was that based on the current period's PPM, which was not the relevant deflator when the PPM changed. In the present case, however, we are dealing with an unchanging PPM. In any event, given that a Paasche index is to be constructed, as is the current actual practice, the present problem must be met; further, as already remarked, the same problem arises for a Laspeyres deflator in the case of disappearing goods.

[39] Note that because the Paasche index bounds the national output deflator based on today's PPM, the deflator in question is described in a way opposite to that which we have generally employed.

[40] Of course, this is the demand reservation price which would have obtained yesterday had today's tastes been in effect. In the case of a good which *disappears* for reasons of demand, a similar recommendation applies to the construction of a Laspeyres cost-of-living index bounding from above the true index constructed with yesterday's indifference map.

[41] Note that a quality improvement—in the sense of more resources embodied in the new variety than in the old—corresponds to a *decrease* in b or an increase in a. This is as it should be. Greater quantities of the old variety than of the new could be produced, other things equal.

[42] A similar remark obviously holds if the new variety embodies fewer resources than the old and the price is to be adjusted upward.

[43] The cases for the cost-of-living index studied in Essay I, unrealistic as they were there, are hopelessly so in the present context. They would involve a quality change in the first good which, from the point of view of resource utilization, would be equivalent to a Hicks-neutral technological change in the production function of some *other* good. Further, if constant returns were imposed, that change would have to be independent of the amount of production of the first good, which is ridiculous. A wholly different approach is clearly required.

REFERENCES FOR ESSAY II

Bergson, A. 1961. *The Real National Income of Soviet Russia since 1928.* Harvard University Press, Cambridge, Massachusetts.

Debreu, G. 1951. "The coefficient of resource utilization," *Econometrica* **19** (3), 273–292.

——. 1954. "Numerical representations of technical change," *Metroeconomica* **6** (2), 45–54.

Fisher, F. M., and Shell, K. 1968. "Taste and quality change in the pure theory of the true cost-of-living index." In *Value, Capital and Growth: Papers in Honour of Sir John Hicks* (J. N. Wolfe, ed.). University of Edinburgh Press, Edinburgh. Also appearing as Essay I in this monograph.

Muellbauer, J. N. J. 1971. "The 'pure theory of the national output deflator' revisited," Warwick Economic Research Papers No. 16, University of Warwick, England.

Moorsteen, R. 1961. "On measuring productive potential and relative efficiency," *Quarterly Journal of Economics* **75** (3), 451–467.

Richter, M. 1966. "Invariance axioms and economic indexes," *Econometrica* **34** (4), 739–755.

Rybczynski, T. M. 1955. "Factor endowment and relative commodity prices," *Economica* **22**, 336–341.

Samuelson, P. A. 1947. *Foundations of Economic Analysis.* Harvard University Press, Cambridge, Massachusetts.

——. 1953–1954. "Prices of factors and goods in general equilibrium," *Review of Economic Studies* **21** (1), 1–20.

Uzawa, H. 1963. "On a two-sector model of economic growth: II," *Review of Economic Studies* **30** (2), 105–118.

von Hofsten, E. A. G. 1952. *Price Indexes and Quality Changes.* Bokförlaget Forum, Stockholm.

Index

Aggregation, 107
Arrow, K. J., 41, 42

Bardhan, P., 111
Bergson, A., 107

Capital intensities, 77–80
  crossing of, 80, 110
  equal, 78
Capital-labor ratio, change in, 78
  effective, 80
Chang, W. W., 110
Constant returns, 73, 76–80, 83–97
Constraint locus, 5
Consumer price index, 59
Corner solutions, in cost-of-living
    index, 23–27
  effect on national output deflator,
    99–105
  in production, 95
Cost-of-living index, 58–59
  construction of, 22
  corner solutions, see Corner solutions
  interior solutions, 8–23
Court, A. T., 38
Cramer's rule, 95

Demand reservation price, in cost-of-
    living index 25, 26
  in national output deflator, 102–104
Disappearing goods, definition of, 24
  effect on cost-of-living index, 24
  effect on national output deflator,
    99–105
Duality, 86

Econometric supply studies, 68
Efficiency units, see Utility efficiency
    units
  in production, 78, 80

Elasticity of factor substitution, 94–95
Elasticity of output supply, 67–75
  gross, 67–73
  net, 68–75
Enthoven, A., 41, 42
Envelope theorem, 13–14, 41, 66, 79, 82,
    90–92, 98–99
Euler's Theorem, 96
External economies, 63
  in production, 63

Factor-augmenting technological
    change, 75–97
  differing rates of augmentation,
    93–97
  in every production function, 90–91
  general case, 81–93
  in single production function, 89–92
  in single sector, 93–97
Factor dosage, 51
  marginal cost of, 64, 65
  vector of marginal, 65
Factor intensities, 81, 88
Factor-intensity matrix, 88
Factor price equalization, 88
Factor requirements function, 51
Factor supplies, changes in, 75–97
  fixed, 102
  inelastic, 63
Fisher, F. M., 43, 49, 107

General equilibrium, 68, 103
Geographical comparisons, 56
Global result, 70, 86
GNP deflator, 50, 59
Griliches, Z., 38
Gross complement, 19–22
  in production, 70
Gross national product, see GNP
Gross substitute, 19–22
  in production, 70

Hedonic price indices, 38, 42
Hicks-neutral technological change,
    63–75, 107
Homotheticity, 20
Houthakker, H. S., 8

Indices of national output, 50
Indifference map, indifference between
    hypothetical price-income
    situations, 4–5
  shifts in, 2
Indirect utility function, 8
Inflationary bias, 58–59
Intensive units, 76
Intertemporal comparisons of welfare,
    2–8
  asymmetry of time, 6
Invention, 100
Investment, 78
Isomorphism, 49, 100
  between pure theory of true cost-of-
    living index and pure theory of
    true national output deflator, 65–66

Kuhn–Tucker–Lagrange, 42

Labor-augmenting technological
    change, 93–97
Labor force, change in, 78
Lancaster, K., 38
Laspeyres index, construction of, 22
  lower bound on true national output
    deflator, 59
  parametrized taste change, 7
  price index, 20, 21, 57–59, 71–73, 86,
    101, 109, 111
  quantity index, 57–59, 109, 111
  upper bound on true cost-of-living
    index, 7, 25, 26
Leontief, W. W., 33, 34, 36

Malmquist, S., 40
Many-sector model, 81–93
Marginal utility of income, 10, 14,
    15, 30
Market imperfections, 59–61
Money output deflator, 53
Moorsteen, R., 107

National output deflator, 50
  arithmetic properties of, 50
Net complement, 19, 23

Net substitute, 19, 23
New goods, 23–27
  definition of, 24
  effect on national output deflator,
    99–105
  for reasons of demand, 100–103
  for reasons of supply, 100–104
Nonsatiation, 24

Opportunity locus, 5

Paasche index, lower bound on true
    cost-of-living index, 7, 25, 26
  overstatement of real output deflator,
    58
  price index, 20, 21, 25, 57–59, 71–73,
    86, 102–105, 109, 111
  quantity index, 57–59, 109, 111
  upper bound on true national output
    deflator, 58, 102
Partial equilibrium, 68
Perfect competition, 59
Planning, 57
Price elasticity of demand, 17, 19–22
Production indices, relevance of, 56–57
Production possibility frontier, 50
Production possibility map, 50–56
  homotheticity of, 51, 53–54, 62–63,
    70–75
Published indices, 58–59
Purchases measured in terms of
    utility efficiency units, 12

Quality change, 27–38
  in construction of national output
    deflator, 105–107
  cross-good effects, 38
  effect on true cost-of-living index, 37
  equivalence to price reduction, 27
  final goods, 29
  good-augmenting type, 27
  intermediate good, 28–29
  local price adjustment for, 27–28
  other price adjustment, 35
  own price adjustment, 29–32
  repackaging case, 27–28, 32–35
  representation as set of price
    adjustments, 37
  service-augmenting type, 27
  variable repackaging, 34
  similarity to embodied
    technological change, 43

Real GNP, 50
Real output deflator, formal description
   of, 61–63
Real output index, formal description
   of, 61–63
Real output indices, 50–56
Richter, M., 50, 107
Rybczynski, T. M., 77, 110

Samuelson, P. A., 39, 41, 66, 107, 111
Shadow price, 101
Shell, K., 49, 107
Slutsky equation, 19, 68
Slutsky's theorem, 17
Specialization, in production, 95
Stone, R., 38
Strotz, R. H., 39
Substitution effects, 69
   in production, 67–75
Substitution elasticity, 110
Substitution terms, symmetry of, 110
Supply elasticities, constant-value, 70
Supply reservation price, in cost-of-
   living index, 25, 26
   in national output deflator, 101–104

Taste change, 8–23, 43
   disembodied, 9, 43
   effect on Laspeyres and Paasche
      indices, 7
   effect on national output deflator, 100
   effect on true cost-of-living index, 11, 20
   embodied, 43

first-order effects of, 19–22
   good-augmenting, 9, 65
   as opposed to quality change, 8–9
   own-augmenting, 26
   second-order effects of, 22–23
Taste change parameter, 65
Technological change, see Hicks-neutral
   technological change
   factor-augmenting, see Factor-
   augmenting technological change,
   Labor-augmenting technological
   change
   general, 97–99
   marginal revenue product of, 98–99
Technological efficiency parameter, 63
True cost-of-living index, base-year
   tastes, 5–6
   comparison of present and past
      constraints, 5
   current tastes, 5–6
   theory of, 2–8
True national output deflator, 65
Two-sector model, 75–93
   comparative statics, 77–78
   outlined, 76

Underemployment, 61
Underutilized resources, 59–61
Utility, comparisons of, 4
Utility efficiency units, 21
   prices per, 13
Uzawa, H., 77, 96, 110, 111

von Hofsten, E. A. G., 2, 25, 40, 107